War after September 11

War after September 11

EDITED BY VERNA V. GEHRING

ROWMAN & LITTLEFIELD PUBLISHERS, INC.
Lanham • Boulder • New York • Oxford

ROWMAN & LITTLEFIELD PUBLISHERS, INC.

Published in the United States of America
by Rowman & Littlefield Publishers, Inc.
A Member of the Rowman & Littlefield Publishing Group
4720 Boston Way, Lanham, Maryland 20706
www.rowmanlittlefield.com

PO Box 317
Oxford
OX2 9RU, UK

British Library Cataloguing in Publication Information Available

Library of Congress Cataloging-in-Publication Data

War after September 11 / edited by Verna V. Gehring.
    p. cm.
    Includes bibliographical references and index.
    ISBN 0-7425-1467-6 (alk. paper) — ISBN 0-7425-1468-4 (pbk. : alk. paper)
    1. War (Philosophy) 2. Terrorism. I. Title: War after September eleven. II. Title:
War after September eleventh. III. Gehring, Verna V.

B105.W3 W37 2002
172'.42—dc21   2002014864

Printed in the United States of America

♾™ The paper used in this publication meets the minimum requirements of American
National Standard for Information Sciences—Permanence of Paper for Printed Library
Materials, ANSI/NISO Z39.48-1992.

Contents

III: Looking Ahead:
The Possibility of a Comprehensive Approach

Preface

Several of the essays in this work appeared as articles in *Philosophy & Public Policy Quarterly*, the journal sponsored by the Institute for Philosophy and Public Policy at the School of Public Affairs, University of Maryland. William A. Galston, Director of the Institute for Philosophy and Public Policy, contributed the introduction, and four of the articles were written by present and former research scholars of the Institute. This volume has benefited from the conversation and thought of all of the research scholars who, during informal paper talks, offered suggestions for improvement of earlier drafts. Thanks must go to David Luban for suggesting the title of this work, and to Carroll Linkins, Demetria Sapienza, and Richard Chapman for their help and kindness in bringing the essays to press.

Special thanks are due to Arthur Evenchik, who served as Editor at the Institute for Philosophy and Public Policy from 1992 to 1999. In editing the *Report from the Institute for Philosophy and Public Policy* (the predecessor to *Philosophy & Public Policy Quarterly*), he commissioned and edited articles that consistently and unfailingly contributed important questions and arguments to public policy debate. Arthur Evenchik serves as an exemplar for the present editor.

Verna V. Gehring
Editor
Institute for Philosophy and Public Policy
School of Public Affairs, University of Maryland
College Park, Maryland

Introduction

William A. Galston

As this book goes to press, the United States is embroiled in a dispute with the government of Afghanistan over civilian casualties incurred during US military operations against the remnants of Taliban and al Qaeda forces operating in that country. Controversy is rising over the treatment of captured "enemy combatants" at the Guantanamo Bay Naval Base and elsewhere. And the US is in the early stages of a great debate, among its citizens and with its allies, over the deployment of its forces to replace Saddam Hussein's regime in Iraq. The Bush administration argues that targeting weapons of mass destruction in the hands of the "axis of evil" represents a logical and necessary expansion of the initial defensive and retaliatory response to the events of September 11; its critics disagree.

These debates raise classic questions of both political prudence and political morality. While not blind to the former, the essays in this volume focus on the latter—the legitimacy of war's ends and war's means. What are the limits of justified retaliation against aggression? What are the morally permissible contours of actions aimed at preventing future aggression? Against whom may campaigns of retaliation and prevention be aimed? Where does nonstate terrorism lie on the continuum from criminality to traditional warfare? Should a state's response to nonstate terrorism be shaped by the paradigm of criminal law, the law of war, or some new blend? How, if at all, should

1

asymmetries of power between states and nonstate actors affect our moral judgment? To what extent should nonmilitary strategies of economic and political development supplement, or supplant, military responses?

The six essays in this volume divide into three pairs. The first pair, by Judith Lichtenberg and Robert Fullinwider, explore the moral challenges posed by terrorism within the traditional paradigms of just war theory and international law. Lichtenberg considers two classic rationales for retaliating against attack—retribution and prevention. Retribution is backward-looking, focusing on the nature of the deed and the identity of the perpetrators. Just retribution is inherently limited, by the need both to demonstrate a "fit" between the provoking deed and the proposed response to it, and also to limit the response, so far as possible, to those who committed the deed. For this reason, Lichtenberg suggests, "despite its usual associations with a certain unflinching hardness, retribution is inadequate to justify the broad actions that have in fact been undertaken since September 11."

The second rationale for retaliation, prevention, is forward-looking rather than backward-looking. The point is not punishing wrongful deeds already committed, but rather reducing as much as possible the chance that anyone will commit such deeds in the future. While prevention is more open-ended than retribution, it is nonetheless limited by moral considerations. One consideration is proportionality: the means employed must be roughly commensurate with the ends sought. If the end is the very survival of a nation and its people, then the scope of legitimate means is wide indeed.

A more significant restraint on wars of prevention is the principle of noncombatant immunity: it is forbidden to target civilians. (This principle rests on the assumption that the distinction between combatants and noncombatants makes empirical and moral sense, an assumption that many terrorists explicitly deny.) This does not mean that military actions resulting in civilian deaths are always wrong. If the planners of the action are aiming at a legitimate military target, and if there is no way to destroy that target without endangering civilians, and if the planners have done everything within reason to avoid civilian casualties, then the action is presumptively legitimate. (In just war theory, this is known as the doctrine of "double effect.") This doctrine rules out not only terrorism explicitly aimed at civilians, but also military action that fails the test of required diligence and caution. Recent American airstrikes in Afghanistan have proved controversial because doubts have been raised about the extent of planners' efforts to minimize what turned out to be significant civilian casualties. For similar reasons, Israel's bombing of an apartment building housing a Hamas terrorist leader, which produced more than a dozen civilian casualties, has raised a domestic as well as international furor.

Properly understood, Lichtenberg concludes, the doctrine of double effect "does not allow people to escape responsibility for the fatal effects of their actions simply by averting their minds. It's not enough not to try to kill civilians; you have to try not to kill them." This may require military officials to increase the risk their own troops must bear in order to reduce the vulnerability of the adversary's civilian population. For example, the higher the altitude from which bombing is undertaken, the lower the risk to pilots, but the greater the chance that minor inaccuracies will produce significant civilian casualties. However reluctant military planners may be to accept an equivalence between the lives of their troops and those of others' civilians, the principle of double effect may require lower-altitude bombing.

Robert Fullinwider begins with a distinction accepted by other contributors to this volume, between judgments of innocence and guilt on the one hand, and combatant versus noncombatant status on the other. In reflecting on legitimate uses of military force, it is the latter that counts rather than the former. But matters are more complex than this straightforward point would suggest. As Fullinwider points out, the laws of war and the distinctions they draw reflect the existence and interests of "states." These laws strictly prohibit nonstate actors from using force to vindicate their demands, however just those demands may be. This prohibition stands in tension, not only with widely held moral intuitions about just revolutions, but also with the fundamental right of self-determination recognized and codified by the United Nations.

Whatever its shortcomings in practice, Fullinwider suggests, it is international law that offers our best chance of escaping anarchy. The problem with the state of nature isn't the absence of morality, but rather of law. Individuals substitute their private moral judgments, and private action to vindicate those judgments, for the shared understandings and collective sanctions of the law—with predictably disastrous effects. "What is scary about terrorists," Fullinwider strikingly asserts, is that "they appeal to morality without appealing to law."

But is it reasonable to expect terrorists (or self-interested state actors, for that matter) to appeal to law? Granted, the analogy between domestic and international law is far from perfect, for a host of familiar reasons. Nonetheless, Fullinwider insists, it would be a grave mistake to ignore international law altogether. The key principle, established at the Nuremberg tribunal after World War II, is that state sovereignty is not absolute: "No state can take complete refuge in Private Judgment. Ultimately, states must face the bar of collective judgment and justify their violent conduct in terms acceptable to the common moral sense of mankind." Moral consistency as well as farsighted prudence demands that the US employ this principle as a maxim of its international conduct. If we are to successfully condemn the exercise of private moral judgment by terrorists and rogue states, we cannot claim the right of private moral judgment whenever it appears to suit our short-term convenience. If we are to reap the advantages of international law, we must accept its constraints.

The second pair of essays explores the possibility that terrorism carried out in contemporary circumstances cannot be addressed adequately within existing paradigms of just war and international law. Paul Kahn begins with distinctions between judgments of guilt or innocence and combatant as opposed to noncombatant status. Combatants are not (necessarily) guilty of anything. Rather, they act in self-defense toward one another. Actions undertaken in legitimate self-defense require the "reciprocal imposition of risk." For this reason, soldiers cannot rightly engage in civilian reprisals or threaten family members of enemy soldiers to induce their surrender.

The centrality of reciprocity, Kahn suggests, has important implications for the use of American power. Reciprocal vulnerability disappears when asymmetries of power are so pronounced that one side can proceed risklessly vis-à-vis the other. If combatants are no longer a threat, then the distinction between combatants and noncombatants loses its moral force. (Consider, for example, high-tech weapons launched from a great distance, beyond the reach of enemy responses.) Under these circumstances, war must give way to policing, where traditional norms of individual moral guilt determine the legitimate objects and means of force. This is not the only "paradox" of riskless warfare. Vast asymmetries in conventional military forces create incentives for the use of unconventional tactics, including terrorism, if the weaker party sees that no other strategy is likely to prove effective. "For the asymmetrically powerful to insist on the maintenance of the combatant/noncombatant distinction," Kahn suggests, "has the appearance of self-serving moralizing." Kahn does not explicitly answer the question of whether this appearance is grounded in reality. Despite the understandable resentment of less powerful nations and peoples, it might nonetheless be the case that the prohibition against terrorism retains its moral force, even though it removes a key weapon from the depleted arsenals of the weak. Finally, asymmetrical power presents a temptation for empire—the use of power restrained only by the self-interest and moral understanding of the preponderantly strong. But asymmetry, Kahn argues, "places a particular burden on any decision to use force. As the asymmetry increases, so does our need to find the grounds for a common belief in the legitimacy of the deployment." The difficulty today is this: The US has something close to a monopoly of global enforcement power, but without the collectively acknowledged legitimacy of the Hobbesian sovereign. This suggests that the US has a moral as well as practical need to find ways of deploying its power that enhance rather than diminish the perceived legitimacy of its use. It is unlikely that a reputation for unilateralism will fortify this perception. Like Kahn, David Luban uses the basic distinction between military and police power to analyze and judge the US response to September 11. The "war model" and the "law model," he argues, are fundamentally different. Each has a well-developed catalogue of permissions and prohibitions; each possesses an internal coherence and integrity; but they rest on different bases and embody divergent maxims of action. In war, as opposed to law, it is permissible to use lethal force on enemy troops regardless of their personal actions; to engage in actions where "collateral damage" is expected; to proceed on the basis of plausible intelligence rather than proof; and to act on the basis of expectations of future enemy action, not only past deeds. Conversely, in war as opposed to law, it is legitimate for enemy combatants to fight back, and prisoners of war who are hors du combat are entitled to a range of legal protections governing their treatment and restricting the ends and means of permissible interrogation. Luban argues that the US government has declined to choose between the war model and the law model, constructing instead a hybrid war-law approach that deprives captured combatants and suspects of nearly all rights. "In line with the war model, they lack the usual rights of criminal suspects—the presumption of innocence, the right to a hearing to determine guilt, the opportunity to prove that the authorities have grabbed the wrong man. But in line with the law model, they are considered unlawful combatants, because they are not uniformed forces, and therefore they lack the rights of prisoners of war. . . . Neither criminal suspects nor POWs, neither fish nor fowl, they inhabit a limbo of rightlessness."

To be sure, there is an argument for this novel hybrid approach. Terrorism combines elements of crime and war, and it poses a unique and heightened danger—especially if terrorists come to possess portable weapons of mass destruction. Under circumstances of "dire menace," it is appropriate to treat terrorists as though they embody the "most dangerous aspects of both warriors and criminals." Luban argues, however, that the case against the hybrid approach is stronger: The law model grows out of relationships within states, while the war model arises from relationships between states. The law model presupposes a community of values, while the war model acknowledges that human beings do not live in a single community with shared norms. The theoretical objection to the hybrid approach is that it is "unprincipled to wrench [these models] apart and recombine them simply because it is in America's interest to do so." The practical objection is that because the war on terrorism (unlike traditional war) has no clear definition of victory or point of termination, the abrogation of human rights inherent in the hybrid model may well be indefinite rather than temporary.

The final set of essays asks whether the US response to terrorism should be predominantly military and if not, what a more comprehensive response might look like. Lloyd Dumas explores the efficacy of economic and political development as part of a counter-terrorism strategy. Scholars who are dubious about this strategy point to the fact that most of the September 11 perpetrators were members of the educated middle class. Dumas does not regard this fact as dispositive. After all, he argues, terrorist groups must recruit new members and appeal to a broader public, both of which goals are promoted if the terrorists can represent themselves as the "avengers of some great wrong, the voice of the voiceless, soldiers for the weak and oppressed." Their capacity to do this successfully is not independent of actual conditions, in particular, economic deprivation and political humiliation. The best response to deprivation is economic development; the best response to humiliation is political recognition. This does not mean that all terrorist groups should be given full official status. It does mean that allowing a wide range of groups with real political agendas to get a hearing would tend to diffuse the feelings of frustration and marginalization that lead some to commit terrorism and others to support it. (Although Dumas does not make the point explicitly, his recommendation is consistent with the oft-heard argument that the repression of domestic dissent in much of the Islamic world deflects discontent toward foreign targets—especially Israel and the US—and creates a more supportive climate for terrorism than would otherwise exist.)

The point, Dumas concludes, is not simply to append development to a military response to terrorism but to undertake development with the right tools and in the right spirit. The right tools take assistance to the grassroots, for example, through microlending. The right spirit eschews top-down thinking and focuses instead on giving disadvantaged and disaffected peoples a sense of "empowerment, self-worth, dignity and respect." Without in any way excusing terrorist acts against innocent civilians, Dumas' argument invites us to make the phenomena of humiliation and recognition more central to our moral understanding of terrorism as well as to our strategic response.

Like Dumas, Benjamin Barber endorses the prudent use of military force against terrorism; like Dumas, he deplores the tendency of some American policymakers to regard such force as an adequate response. The resort to terrorism, he argues, arises from the perception of some groups that they are powerless; in particular, that they lack democratic options. In substantial measure, terrorism is a product of what he terms the "global democracy deficit"—not only the absence of democratic institutions in nations that spawn terrorists, but also the failure (for which the US must accept its share of responsibility) to construct transnational democratic institutions capable of containing and domesticating global anarchy. Starting in the seventeenth century, philosophers and political leaders used the idea of the "social contract" to build nation-states whose sovereignty could tame the domestic anarchy of religious war. But this centuries-old formula of tranquility within states and anarchy among them will no longer suffice. Like the individuals and religious communities of the seventeenth century, today's nations must surrender a portion of their independence to achieve sustainable security and the conditions for living decent lives. Democracy can no longer survive, nation by nation. We must acknowledge the need for, and move toward, an unprecedented global "Declaration of Interdependence."

Barber focuses on unregulated global markets as a principal source of global anarchy. Not only does this market disempower economically weaker states; it is also experienced as a cultural assault on

traditional communities and religion itself. In some part, violent fundamentalism represents a defensive reaction to aggressive materialism. If we rightly deplore the omnivorous politics we call totalitarianism, or the omnivorous religion we call theocracy, then we should also
and equally deplore the omnivorous market that creates a "novel bottom-up form of totalizing homogeneity" that is deeply threatening to
cultural and religious diversity. Global democracy will require a global
civic faith, but that faith cannot impose secularism or encode hostili-
ty to religion. "We cannot secure the liberty of the public square,"
Barber insists, by "driving the faithful of every religion from it." The
future of global democracy rests on a principled middle way between
theocracy and a forcible privatization of religion that denies the public and communal dimensions of faith. If we are wise and farsighted,
if we bring all mankind within the sphere of democracy and create
institutions that tame the anarchy of global markets, we will make a
world in which "both liberty and faith are secured" and in which "terrorism becomes irrelevant."

Taken together, the essays in this volume invite Americans to
think broadly about the just aims and legitimate limits of their country's role in the world. The United States is the most dominant force—
militarily, economically, and culturally—in the world today, by some
estimates the most dominant nation in human history. How will it use
that power? The United States has an opportunity to respond to an
unjust attack in ways that enhance the longterm prosperity and stability of other nations as well as its own security. Depending on the
course of action it adopts, the United States can either fortify or weaken
the tentative movement of recent decades toward a more law-like
international order.

With great power, in short, comes great responsibility. When
external restraints are weak, self-restraint is essential. In the words of
Shakespeare,

> O! it is excellent to have a giant's strength, but it is tyrannous to use
> it like a giant.

Traditional Paradigms and their Limits

I

The Ethics of Retaliation

Judith Lichtenberg

From the very first hours after the September 11 attacks on New York and Washington, President Bush vowed to retaliate against those responsible. The American public supported him overwhelmingly, and continues to do so. But what does retaliation mean, and what does it allow? What kinds of actions are appropriate, and on what basis can we justify them? Some people will be impatient with such questions—feeling that, in the wake of these wrenching events, justification is either unnecessary or plain obvious. But the risks surrounding what we do—or fail to do—are great, so it is worth thinking about the moral dimensions of our responses.

Two Rationales for Retaliation

Philosophers have traditionally distinguished between two different sorts of justifications for retaliation or punishment. One is "backward-looking," the other "forward-looking." The backward-looking approach looks to what has already happened: it justifies retaliation purely in terms of the justice of meting out punishment to one who has deliberately caused harm to others. This rationale, which philosophers call *deontological* (from the Greek word for necessity), is often linked with the popularly expressed goals of retribution, revenge, vengeance, an eye for an eye. The idea is that one who does harm

11

deserves to suffer, that punishment is just and even necessary to "right the wrong" and restore the moral balance. The terrorists, like other criminals, must be brought to justice; justice must be brought to the terrorists.

To describe this approach as backward-looking is not to criticize it. It is only to recognize that what justifies retribution is not any supposed good consequences, such as deterring similar acts in the future, but simply that the guilty party has done wrong and deserves to pay. From the point of view of retribution, it doesn't matter if any further good comes of punishment; punishing the guilty is inherently right and just, and that's all it needs to be. Forward-looking justifications, by contrast, are *consequentialist:* they justify punishment or retaliation as a means of bringing about some supposed good consequences, such as preventing or deterring further violence, or (in some cases) reforming or rehabilitating the wrongdoer.

Our institutions of punishment generally combine a backward-looking retributivist justification and forward-looking consequentialist ones. Most people find the retributivist argument compelling: they think that it's inherently wrong for people to get away with murder and that we must serve justice by giving people what they deserve. But it is clear that we do, and must, inflict punishment also for forward-looking reasons: primarily to remove dangerous people from society (domestic or international) so they can do no further harm, and to send a message to other potential criminals that such behavior will not be tolerated. We can think of these forward-looking considerations—sometimes called specific and general deterrence, respectively—broadly in terms of self-defense. It's hard to imagine a system that didn't combine backward-looking with forward-looking elements.

Retribution: A Closer Look

But matters are more complicated than these remarks might suggest, as we can see if we examine the notion of retribution more carefully. Note first that retribution is popularly associated with revenge and vengeance, which, despite their near-universality as emotions and motives to action, have some explaining to do. Two wrongs, we know, don't make a right, so retributivists have to explain why the second "wrong" is *not* wrong and thus *can* make a right. Typically they do this by invoking the idea of balance, of inflicting suffering on the criminal as a counterweight to the suffering he inflicted on the victim—something that raises the victim's stature to what it was before the crime, or that lowers the wrongdoer's to what, in light of his crime, it should be.

Revenge also suggests the unleashing of powerful emotions that may not be easily contained: the punishment may exceed the crime, and violence may continue and even escalate. The Hatfields and the McCoys, the Israelis and the Palestinians. Defenders of retribution answer this objection by distancing it from its suspect cousins revenge and vengeance. Two features can tame retribution and render it respectable. One is the idea that the punishment must fit the crime, an idea that is essential to retribution but not necessarily to the emotionally-based revenge and vengeance. And while it is common to emphasize that the punishment must be severe enough to fit the crime, it is equally crucial, retributivists insist, that punishment not exceed the crime in severity.

Furthermore, while the principle of retribution says that the guilty must be punished, equally important is its demand that *only* the guilty may be punished. Punishment must be tailored to reach those who have done wrong and leave untouched those who have not.

Despite these crucial qualifications, retribution still seems to some people pointless and incomprehensible. Why add injury to injury? Unless punishment does some good, what rationale can be given for it? Ironically, when we consider crimes on the scale of the September 11 attacks, retribution can seem especially meaningless. Many of the criminals are already dead, and moreover they and their allies seem not to regard death—for most of us the worst punishment—as punishment at all. Even if they did, the deaths (or other punishment) of a few score guilty murderers pale in comparison with the crimes they have committed.

Yet most people find in the idea of retribution something satisfying and morally sound. Clearly they are more justified in this opinion once the strict requirements of retribution are understood. The fit of punishment to crime (not too little, not too much) and the requirement of guilt transform retribution from a potentially brutal idea to one constrained by strict limits. Indeed, the principle of retribution can be conceived to be as much about the limits of punishment as about its necessity. So it's not as ironic as it may seem that, despite its usual associations with a certain unflinching hardness, retribution is inadequate to justify the broad actions that have in fact been undertaken since September 11. These actions and their clearly foreseeable consequences—the waging of war and the suffering and hardship it imposes on many people not guilty of terrorism—are much too indiscriminate to be justified in terms of retribution.

Making the World Safe

But retribution is only part of what the current retaliation efforts— and most retaliation efforts—are about. Here we may note a certain ambiguity in the word "retaliation." Much of the post-September 11 rhetoric suggests that the goal of retaliation is identical with the goal of bringing the terrorists to justice. But clearly there is another goal: to reduce the threat of terrorist attacks as much as possible. We retaliate not only to punish, but also to prevent: to disable potential terrorists from successful action, to deter them if possible, to make the world safe from terrorist violence. Indeed, even those who care nothing for retribution are concerned about prevention. We are engaged in acts of collective self-defense.

Few people would disagree that preventing such violence is a legitimate and worthy goal. But prevention raises questions very different from those confronted by retribution. One is *how* to prevent such violence. We know much better how to punish than how to prevent. If, as some people argue, violence breeds violence, then war is not the way to achieve our goals. Even if this pacifist view is wrong, the policy of employing war as a tool involves countless guesses and gambles about just which of myriad possible causal chains our actions will set off. It thus raises empirical questions whose answers we can never be certain of. Retribution, by contrast, raises no comparable questions of fact.

But the goal of prevention also raises an explicitly moral question: what means may be employed to prevent terrorism? We can imagine extinguishing it by indulging in a degree of violence that would be excessive and reprehensible. "By any means necessary" is not an adequate answer.

Despite its harsh reputation, the principle of retribution imposes strict moral limits—the requirement to punish only the guilty and to do so in proportion to the crime. But it's not clear what limits the goal of prevention imposes. It suggests only that the actions contemplated have the desired effect, and that could sanction the unleashing of great brutality and violence. In the domestic context, the preventive aims of the criminal justice system are for the most part constrained by respect for the civil rights and liberties of American citizens. Excessive and invasive means to prevent or reduce crime would evoke sharp reactions from many quarters. But when the goal of preventing violence involves action beyond our borders, respect for the rights and welfare of other countries' people looms much less important—if it figures at all.

Just war theory—the accumulated body of thought regarding the moral constraints on the conduct of war—offers two relevant principles. One is the principle of proportionality. The other is the principle of noncombatant immunity.

Proportionality demands that we weigh means against ends. Which ends justify which means? When a country is attacked, and the end in question is a nation's survival or the survival of its people, proportionality may seem to rule out very little. For what can be a more worthy or legitimate end? Spelling out the meaning of proportionality, the nineteenth century philosopher Henry Sidgwick argued that in the conduct of war it is not permissible to do "any mischief which does not tend materially to the end [of victory], nor any mischief of which the conduciveness to the end is slight in comparison with the amount of the mischief." As Michael Walzer points out, Sidgwick's argument seems to rule out only purposeless or wanton violence. Although, as Walzer also notes, in war this is no small achievement, still it does not take us very far in limiting the conduct of war.

Noncombatant Immunity

Much more central to limiting the destructiveness of war is the principle of noncombatant immunity. The core idea is that in war one may not target civilians. In keeping with this principle, President Bush at the beginning of the war in Afghanistan made "low collateral damage"—the military euphemism for civilian casualties—a criterion for the conduct of the war. At the same time, since September 11 a large majority of the American public has favored military action even if it means the killing of civilians.

The *Washington Post* reported that "as many as 10 times" in October and November "the Air Force believed it had top Taliban and al Qaeda members in its cross hairs in Afghanistan but was unable to receive clearance to fire in time to hit them because of a cumbersome approval process" and disagreements with the US Central Command "over how much weight to give to concerns about avoiding civilian casualties." Now it's clear that at least part of the reason for American leaders' concern about protecting noncombatants is strategic. They understand the importance of winning—certainly of not losing—the war for public opinion in the Muslim world. They know that nothing is more likely to turn opinion further against the United States, and to disturb the fragile relationships the US has with its Islamic allies, than the killing of civilians. But even this strategic reason rests at bottom on a moral one: it is because people believe it is morally wrong to kill noncombatants that it is useful to respect the prohibition. There is another important moral consideration: our condemnation of terrorist attacks on civilians would ring hollow if we ourselves committed such acts.

But the principle of noncombatant immunity raises several questions. First, how should we draw the line between those who are legitimate targets of military attack and those who are not? Second—and this question is inseparable from the first—*why* should we draw such a distinction? Third, just what does the principle of noncombatant immunity prohibit and what does it allow?

In ordinary discourse we often use the terms "noncombatants," "civilians," and "innocent people" synonymously. What makes such people morally immune from attack? In "War, Innocence, and Terrorism," and elsewhere, Robert Fullinwider has noted an important ambiguity in the word "innocent." We tend to use the word to mean "morally guiltless" or "morally good." In this sense it is clear that the distinction between combatants and noncombatants is perfectly distinct from the class of noninnocents and innocents. Some combatants are morally good, some noncombatants are morally bad. Some conscripts are unwilling soldiers who do not support their country's cause; some civilians applaud their country's murderous actions from the sidelines. But the relevant meaning of "innocence" in war, Fullinwider suggests, has to do with the absence or presence of threateningness, not moral guilt. Typically, combatants are threats—they have and use weapons to try and kill their enemies—while noncombatants are not. It is because they are nonthreatening, not because they are morally innocent, that noncombatants are morally immune from attack.

It's easy to confuse moral guilt and threateningness, because in typical crimes the two go together. The ordinary murderer threatens his victim, and he is morally guilty. But in war and some other situations the two concepts can come apart. Philosophers once had to dream up fantastic examples to illustrate this point, but recent events have rendered the examples merely realistic. Passengers on the planes that crashed into the World Trade Center were what philosophers call innocent threats or shields. Through no fault of their own, they threatened the lives of those in the buildings. It is plausible to think that if government officials could have prevented the deaths of thousands inside the buildings by shooting down the planes, they would have been justified in doing so. The passengers on the plane (minus the terrorists) were—we may suppose—morally unstained, but they posed a mortal threat to the lives of other people, and this rendered them legitimate targets.

So we can draw the line between legitimate and illegitimate targets via the notion of a threat. Combatants are ordinarily armed and threatening, noncombatants are not. (There will, of course, be borderline and unclear cases.) Another basis for the distinction can be found in an intriguing discussion by the philosopher George Mavrodes. Mavrodes argues that the distinction between combatants and noncombatants depends not on an intrinsic moral difference between the two groups but on a convention: a pragmatic calculation that in the long run less carnage and destruction will result if we limit battle to a circumscribed class of people. It's as if warmakers got together and agreed that they could achieve the same goals at lesser cost by playing the war game in a restricted rather than an unlimited way, declaring some people players and others off limits. More specifically still, we can imagine the leaders of each nation consenting to such an agreement on the grounds that if they vowed not to target the other side's civilians, their enemies might do so as well.

The idea that war is a rule-governed activity and not a free-for-all has always seemed somewhat strange, but the conduct of states in the international arena shows that, fortunately, it is accepted most of the time. The particular rule limiting combat to agreed-upon players is one of the most important, preventing war from infiltrating every corner of people's lives.

So we find two bases for the immunity of noncombatants: one resting on threateningness as the central justification for violence in war, and the other on a pragmatic calculation that a rule protecting noncombatants can reduce the carnage and destruction of war. Still, war is messy, and inevitably military actions will sometimes kill civilians. And so the question is how to decide when such actions are justified.

The Doctrine of Double Effect

Catholic theologians in the Middle Ages devised the "doctrine of double effect" to answer this question. According to the doctrine, it is never permissible to kill civilians directly; one may never aim at or intend their deaths. But suppose some civilians are killed in the course of a legitimate military operation—an operation directed only at a military target. Suppose also that one knows or foresees that they will be killed. Whereas intending to kill civilians is never permissible, according to the doctrine of double effect, foreseeing civilian deaths as an effect of a permissible action (such as aiming at a military target) is not prohibited.

A great deal has been written both defending and criticizing the doctrine of double effect. On the one hand, much about the doctrine seems highly suspect and sophistical, and almost all the examples used to illustrate it outside the war context (concerning abortion and euthanasia, for example) only heighten that suspicion. On the other hand, its use in making moral distinctions in war seems almost indispensable. Military personnel intend to hit military targets, but they know that some civilians in the surrounding area will be hit as well. If killing civilians were sufficient to render such missions morally impermissible, wars could not be fought. But wars will be fought and must be fought; therefore some way of making the distinction must be allowed.

Michael Walzer has done much to remove the aura of sophistry surrounding the doctrine of double effect. The original doctrine distinguishes between an action one intends (say, the bombing of a munitions factory) and an effect one foresees as the result of this action (say, the killing of civilians who live in the neighborhood). It says that the action is allowable, as long as you don't intend the other effect—the deaths of the civilians. But as Walzer argues,

> Simply not to intend the death of civilians is too easy; most often, under battle conditions, the intentions of soldiers are focused narrowly on the enemy. What we look for in such cases is some sign of a positive commitment to save civilian lives. . . . And if saving civilian lives means risking soldiers' lives, the risk must be accepted.

To illustrate the point, Walzer recounts a World War I soldier's story: when they were about to toss a bomb into a cellar or dugout, he and his comrades would first shout down to make sure no civilians were inside, thereby jeopardizing their own safety.

Walzer's proviso saves the doctrine of double effect from abuse and trivialization. Properly understood, the doctrine does not allow people to escape responsibility for the fatal effects of their actions simply by averting their minds. It's not enough not to try to kill civilians; you have to try *not* to kill them.

How hard do you have to try? How radical Walzer's proviso is depends on how great the risks we think soldiers must take to minimize civilian casualties. Walzer doesn't say, and clearly there is no simple answer. But it is crucial to see that his proviso requires *our* soldiers taking risks to protect *their* civilians. Given the chauvinism that often comes in war's wake, that sounds like a radical idea.

What justifies it? If all human beings are equal, it may be argued that our people are no more valuable than their people and that therefore we must treat human beings without regard to nationality. But few will be convinced by such reasoning, especially in times of war. More persuasive is a Mavrodes-like pragmatic account of the rules of war. Mavrodes's argument suggests that the best way to avoid annihilation is to observe certain rules—against targeting civilians, in favor of protecting civilians, against nuclear, chemical, and biological weapons—and to treat these rules as nearly sacred. They are not in fact sacred—their justification is largely consequentialist—but the risks that come with their violation are so great that we are better off treating them as more than rules of convenience.

There are other reasons to observe such rules as well. One is the sort of strategic consideration mentioned earlier. Appearing to be sensitive to humanitarian concerns is an important element in persuading the international community, especially those inclined to distrust us, that we are not simply self-interested. We need to ensure that our actions don't create more terrorists than they destroy. But it's not simply a matter of appearances. It's crucial that our conduct not blur the line between ourselves and those we condemn. If we abandon the moral high ground, we risk corrupting the standards that render our country worth defending.

Sources

Robert Fullinwider, "War and Innocence," *Philosophy & Public Affairs*, vol. 5 (1975) and "Terrorism, Innocence, and War," *Philosophy & Public Policy Quarterly*, vol. 21, no. 4; Judith Lichtenberg, "War, Innocence, and the Doctrine of Double Effect, *Philosophical Studies*, vol. 74 (1994); George Mavrodes, "Conventions and the Morality of War," *Philosophy & Public Affairs*, vol. 4 (1975); Thomas E. Ricks, "Target Approval Delays Cost Air Force Key Hits," *Washington Post* (November 18, 2001); Henry Sidgwick, *Elements of Politics*; Michael Walzer, *Just and Unjust Wars* (Basic Books, 1977).

Terrorism, Innocence, and War

Robert K. Fullinwider

The events of September 11, 2001 defy the power of words to describe, console, or even explain. Nevertheless, because the United States must respond in one way or another, and because people must give or withhold their support to any national course of action, words necessarily come into play, words to formulate goals and words to justify the means to achieve them. "Terrorism" is one of the words ubiquitous in the aftermath of September 11, "war" another.

Carlin Romano, a philosopher and critic, writes in the *Chronicle of Higher Education* that a third word, "innocence," should get more attention than it has received. The "clarification and defense of innocence" by intellectuals, social commentators, and public officials, Romano believes, could add an important element to the fight against terrorism.

Innocence

"Innocence" links "war" and "terrorism." Terrorists are counted as murderers because they kill the innocent. Similarly, in war, military forces are prohibited by common custom and international law from targeting civilians. This prohibition "assumes innocence at its core," notes Romano. Perhaps so, but not "innocence" in the sense that underwrites Romano's initial condemnation of terrorists.

Romano insists that terrorism cannot be justified morally, no matter what its political aims, because terrorists select their victims haphazardly, without concern for innocence or guilt. Here, he construes "innocence" under a model of crime and punishment. On that model, punishment should fall on the guilty, not the innocent, on the wrongdoer, not the mere bystander. Just punishment, accordingly, must allow for some sort of antecedent "due process," in which individuals are found guilty according to evidence and only then subjected to penalties in proper proportion to their wrongs. Since the terrorist kills "haphazardly," he doesn't fulfill this minimal demand of just punishment.

In war, however, the notion of "innocence" has nothing to do with lack of blameworthiness. Rather, it divides individuals into two classes: those who may be directly targeted by military force and those who may not. The former includes uniformed armed forces (combatants), the latter ordinary civilians (noncombatants). This division derives not from the imperatives of crime and punishment but from the imperatives of self-defense. In resisting aggression, a state may direct lethal force against the agency endangering it, and that agency is the military force of the aggressor.

From the point of view of moral-wrongdoing and just punishment, many of the aggressor's military personnel may be innocent; they may be reluctant conscripts with no sympathy for their nation's actions. Likewise, among ordinary civilians, many may actively support and favor their country's criminal aggression. They are not innocent. But *from the point of view of self-defense,* the moral quality of the conscript's reluctance and the civilian's enthusiasm is not relevant. What matters is that the former is a combatant, the latter not.

Consequently, war must be prosecuted by means that discriminate between the two classes. Specifying membership in the two classes is, of course, a difficult and somewhat arbitrary affair. Combatants are first of all those in a warring country's military service. They wear uniforms, bear arms, and are trained to be on guard. Because they wield the means of violence and destruction directed at a defending nation, such soldiers are fair targets of lethal response by that nation, even when they are in areas to the rear of active fighting and even when they are sleeping. However, not all enemy soldiers may be attacked. Those rendered *hors de combat* through injury, capture, or some other means possess the same immunities from being killed as civilian noncombatants. Conversely, individuals not in uniform but actively participating in the war effort, such as civilian leaders and managers directing overall military policy, are fair targets of attack. They count as combatants. The operative language in the Geneva Convention of 1949 and in the UN Resolution on Human Rights of 1968—two legal protocols governing the prosecution of war—confers immunity on those "not taking part in hostilities." Obviously, there is plenty of room to construe this phrase in very different ways. Even so, some people—the very old and the very young, for example—clearly qualify for noncombatant immunity on any construal.

While the two points of view—of crime and punishment, on the one hand, and self-defense, on the other—understand "innocence" in different ways, either of them seems clearly to indict the perpetrators of the September 11 attacks. First, those who used hijacked passenger planes as bombs targeted civilians as such, at least in their attack on the World Trade Center. If the attackers considered themselves at war, they violated one of war's laws. Second, the attackers provided no advance notice of their plan to exact punishment from the occupants of the World Trade Center and no forum for the occupants to answer any accusations or charges. If the attackers thought of themselves as avenging angels, they violated due process.

Terrorism

That Osama bin Laden and his network stepped across a clear line marking right from wrong seems signaled by the universal condemnation of the events of September 11. Even the League of Arab States expressed its "revulsion, horror, and shock over the terrorist attacks" against America. Nevertheless, matters may not be as simple as the foregoing account suggests.

First of all, the laws of war and the distinctions they draw are creatures of *states* and *state interests*. Individuals and groups who have no states to represent their grievances, or who stand at odds to the arrangements of power imposed by the prevailing state system, are barred from using violence to vindicate their just demands (as they may see them). Indeed, whatever their cause, they are condemned as criminals if they resort to violence. The UN International Convention for the Suppression of Terrorist Bombings (1997), for example, makes it a crime to explode a lethal device "in a public place" or even to attack a government facility such as an embassy. These acts, it goes on to say, constitute terrorism and "are under no circumstances justifiable by considerations of a political, philosophical, ideological, racial, ethnic, [or] religious . . . nature." No cause however good warrants violent response if the actor is an individual or group, not a state.

Since the United States is a country founded on violent rebellion against lawful authority, we can hardly endorse a blanket disavowal of the right by others violently to rebel against their own oppressors. Indeed, Thomas Jefferson offered a small paean to political violence in letters he sent to Abigail Adams, James Madison, and William Smith in 1787. "I hold that a little rebellion now and then is a good thing," Jefferson wrote, "& as necessary in the political world as storms in the physical. . . . What signify a few lives lost in a century or two? The tree of liberty must be refreshed from time to time with the blood of patriots & tyrants. It is its natural manure." The occasion of Jefferson's letters was the just-suppressed Shay's Rebellion, the violent resistance by desperate farmers in western Massachusetts against the due process of law that, in a time of economic distress, was grinding them into dust. Only a handful of lives were lost in the short affair, but it lent a degree of urgency to delegates from various states scurrying off to Philadelphia to replace the Articles of Confederation.

Nor is Jefferson alone in looking favorably at a "little rebellion" by people who resort to violence in the name of a great cause. John Brown remains for many Americans a martyr in the fight against slavery, though his actions would count as terrorism under contemporary definitions and international conventions. While leading a gang of antislavery guerilla fighters in eastern Kansas in 1855, Brown took revenge for an assault by slavers on the town of Lawrence by dragging five men out of the small proslavery settlement of Pottawatomie Creek one night and hacking them to death. In 1859, in his ill-fated attempt to seize the United States armory at Harper's Ferry, and precipitate (he fancied) a vast slave rebellion, Brown seized sixty hostages from the neighboring precincts.

Killing "innocents"—Brown's victims at Pottawatomie Creek were not accorded any due process, nor were they combatants in uniform—and taking civilian hostages: these are the very deeds deplored and condemned by UN resolutions and conventions. They make Brown a quintessential terrorist. Yet many people refuse to view Brown this way because they don't accept the uncompromising UN position that "irregular" violence—violence initiated by individuals and groups—is "under no circumstances justifiable by considerations of a political, philosophical, ideological, racial, ethnic, [or] religious . . . nature." They believe that in some circumstances a cause

may be sufficiently weighty to justify shedding blood, even "innocent" blood.

So, too, believes the League of Arab States. Though it condemned
the September 11 attack as "terrorism," it refuses to accept an unqual-
ified version of the UN's view that, for example, exploding a lethal
device "in a public place" counts always as terrorism. In its 1998
Convention for the Suppression of Terrorism, the League starts with a
definition pretty much in line with the United Nation's. Terrorism is

> [a]ny act of violence, whatever its motives or purposes, that occurs
> in the advancement of an individual or collective criminal agenda
> and seeking to sow panic among people, causing fear by harming
> them, or placing their lives, liberty or security in danger . . .

A "terrorist offense" is any act in furtherance of a terrorist objective.

So far, so good (though we may wonder about the force of the
modifier "criminal" in reference to the terrorist's "agenda"). But the
Convention then adds:

> All cases of struggle by whatever means, including armed struggle,
> against foreign occupation and aggression for liberation and self-
> determination, in accordance with the principles of international
> law, *shall not be regarded as an offense.*

What does this added qualification mean? Read one way (putting
emphasis on the clause "in accordance with the principles of international law"), it can be taken as proscribing the same deeds outlawed by
UN conventions. Read another way (taking account of the fact that the
definition of "terrorism" is prefaced by an initial affirmation of "the
right of peoples to combat foreign occupation and aggression by whatever means, in order to liberate their territories and secure their right to
self determination"), it can be taken as licensing some irregular violence
(that directed against foreign "occupation" and promoting Arab "self-
determination") while precluding other violence (that on behalf of a
"criminal agenda"). Moreover, the matter is muddied further by the fact
that the UN itself recognizes a fundamental right to self-determination,
a right to resist "colonial, foreign and alien domination." Through
Osama bin Laden's eyes, the attack of September 11 fell upon an alien
dominator of Arabia and bespoke a campaign that would not end
"before all infidel armies leave the land of Muhammed." What could
the right to self-determination mean if it tied one's hands against the
very source of "humiliation and degradation" imposed upon the
Islamic world from the outside for eighty years?

Carlin Romano writes that it probably never occurred to bin Laden "how awful it is to kill innocent people." But bin Laden's own self-justification indicates the contrary. "Millions of innocent children are being killed as I speak," he declared, children who are dying in Iraq as a putative consequence of the economic embargo imposed on that state by an American-led coalition. Osama bin Laden purported to act on behalf of innocence. Why should he not calculate, as Jefferson implied, that shedding the blood of a few now may save the lives and liberty of many others in the long run?

Moreover, why should he feel restrained by the conventional views of innocence? Isn't it arbitrary to immunize from attack people who may be causally implicated in the oppression one is resisting? By convention, the civilians of an aggressor nation who buy their country's war bonds are noncombatants and immune from attack. But without those war bonds, the aggressor nation would not be able to buy the guns and planes and bombs that enable it to prosecute its aggression. Why should those citizens be counted as "innocent" or made immune?

Terrorists, writes Romano, must believe in some "philosophy of innocence, however pinched." They assume the guilt of their victims, but on "transparently flimsy grounds" Obviously, their grounds won't line up with the considerations operative in the conventions of international law, but those conventions weren't endorsed by the terrorists in the first place and don't take their perspectives to heart.

Consider the infamous massacre of Israeli athletes at the 1972 Munich Olympics by Black September, a Palestinian terrorist organization. Weren't those athletes uncontrovertibly innocent? From the point of view of Black September, they were not. They were the knowing and willing representatives of Israel to an international affair where their presence would lend further international credibility and legitimacy to their state. From the point of view of their attackers, the athletes were active and informed accessories to a continuing "crime"—the support of the "criminal" state of Israel. These are not flimsy grounds for charges of "guilt," although they are grounds thoroughly contestable and clearly lying outside the scope of considerations allowed by international law.

The Rule of Law

It is too easy to dismiss the terrorist as evil incarnate, as a demon beyond the human pale. "The terrorist," claims one writer, "represents a new breed of man which takes humanity back to prehistoric times, to the times when morality was not yet born." But this characterization seems wrong. If anything, terrorists are throwbacks to a "prehistoric time" when morality was not yet under control. What is scary about terrorists is that they appeal to morality without appealing to law. They act as a law unto themselves. Let me explain.

Political theorists tell a story about the "State of Nature" to explain and defend government. The State of Nature proves to be intolerable for its inhabitants, whose lives are "solitary, poore, nasty, brutish, and short" (according to Thomas Hobbes). Contrary to common impressions, however, the problem in the State of Nature is not that people are so immoral, so lacking in any sense of justice or decency, that they prey wantonly upon one another. The problem is that people are *so moral,* so determined to vindicate rights or uphold honor at any cost that they become a menace to each other.

The distinctive feature of the State of Nature, as John Locke points out, is not the absence of morality but the absence of *law.* It is a circumstance in which the "law of nature"—the moral law—must be enforced by each individual. Each is responsible for vindicating her own rights and the rights of others. All prosecution of crime and injustice in the State of Nature is freelance. Such a situation is the spawning ground of the never-ending chain of retaliation and counter-retaliation of the blood feud. "For every one in that state being both Judge and Executioner of the Law of Nature, Men being partial to themselves, Passion and Revenge is very apt to carry them too far, and with too much heat, in their own Cases; as well as negligence, and unconcernedness, to make them too remiss, in other Men's."

Even if persons were not biased in their own favor, the problems of enforcing justice in the State of Nature would remain deadly. How would crime be defined? How would evidence for its commission be gathered and validated? Who would be punished, and in what manner? What would constitute legitimate self-defense? Who would calculate the rectification due from unjust aggression? Nothing in the State of Nature ensures any common understanding about these questions. The contrary is the case. Private understanding pitted against private understanding produces an escalation of response and counter-response that lets violence erupt and feed on itself.

The solution, of course, is, as Locke proposed, "an establish'd, settled, known Law, received and allowed by common consent to be the

Standard of Right and Wrong, and the common measure to decide all Controversies," and "a known and indifferent Judge, with Authority to determine all differences according to the established Law." This solution prevails, more or less, in the domestic case. In most states, a common law tolerably resolves disputes, even if that law is not always the product of common consent. The law does not always work well enough, however, and rebellious violence against its inflexibilities and oppressions as often elicits our sympathy as it invokes our fear and antipathy. "Irregular justice"—or vigilantism—can redirect the law toward a more just course. Moreover, sometimes the existing regime of law is so oppressive that outright revolution seems in order. At the end of the eighteenth century, a great many Americans, newly born of their own "revolution," sympathized with the revolution in France that destroyed a decadent monarchy and substituted republicanism; a great many others recoiled in horror at the revolution's excesses as it tumbled into tyranny. In the years since, Americans have both supported and resisted revolutions abroad. Our ambivalence is rooted in twin impulses: to warm to the oppressed in their liberation struggles and to fear the disorder of Private Judgment substituting for law.

At the international level, the rule of law likewise rescues the community of states from intolerable anarchy, though unlike domestic law, international law is a patchwork of treaties, conventions, and understandings among independent actors, each jealous of its sovereignty. Few tribunals exist where "a known and indifferent Judge" possesses full "Authority to determine all differences" among nations; nor is there a common agent of coercion to enforce the judge's rulings on recalcitrant parties. Still, laws and conventions bring some order to international affairs, including the laws of war and the conventions against terrorism referred to earlier. Admittedly, these laws and conventions stack the deck against nonstate actors. And—as the posture of the League of Arab States indicates—some people and some states will want to support nonstate actors in violent response to perceived wrongs and oppressions. But even behind such sympathizing and support lies the worrisome specter of Private Judgment. Osama bin Laden, in his isolated redoubts in the Afghan mountains, elects himself as the vindicator of Islamic honor and rights. He answers to no one or no community but to his own sense of justice. Self-elected vigilantes on the international scene may be tolerated—or even supported—by states when their vigilantism remains a mere thorn in the sides of enemies; but when the vigilantes hold in their hands the power to destroy people by the scores and hundreds of thousands, the face of Private Judgment is hideous even to those who join in its chosen cause. When the League of Arab States proffered its condemnation of the September 11 attacks, it had not suddenly forgotten the experience of eighty years of "humiliation and degradation" noted by bin Laden, it had not suddenly abandoned the cause of Palestinian justice, it had not suddenly converted to nonviolence. Rather, it had suddenly lost its taste for Private Judgment. Osama bin Laden is beholden to no one, not even to the Arab states themselves. Consequently, he is a peril to all.

Private Judgment is not only a menace when exercised by individuals but when exercised by states as well. Countries undermine the efficacy of international law by reserving to themselves Private Judgment about its application. For example, in 1928, Western powers agreed in the Kellogg-Briand Pact to outlaw war as a tool of national policy. They determined that armed aggression was henceforth a crime. But each of the Pact's signatories reserved to itself final judgment about when its acts were proper self-defense and when improper aggression against a neighbor. As a consequence, the Kellogg-Briand Pact inhibited war the way matches inhibit fire.

In the aftermath of World War II, when Nazi leaders were put on trial for war crimes, they interposed a potentially fatal objection: the Nuremberg tribunal before which they appeared had no standing to judge Germany's war policy since the Kellogg-Briand Pact reserved to each country final judgment about whether it was acting lawfully. In rebuttal, the United States joined Great Britain in arguing that although a state may be free in the first instance to decide whether it is acting in self-defense, its exercise of the right of self-defense is nevertheless ultimately subject to review by the international community. Whether this was an ingenious construction of the Kellogg-Briand Pact or an invention from whole cloth, the argument won the day and established an important principle of international law: that no state can take complete refuge in Private Judgment. Ultimately, states must face the bar of collective judgment and justify their violent conduct in terms acceptable to the common moral sense of mankind.

This new principle was an important step for international law, since a system of law in which each party can veto the application of the law to itself is no system of law at all. So long as each party remains the sole judge of its own case, the State of Nature remains in place.

Having struck a notable blow for the principle of law at Nuremberg, the United States has not always honored its own vital handiwork. For example, in 1985, when Nicaragua alleged in the World Court that we were guilty of aggression for supporting the Contras, we did not defend our support by arguing that it constituted collective self-defense. We argued instead an interpretation of the United Nations charter that made the question of whether we were acting in self-defense nonjusticiable. We argued that our actions could be reviewed only by the Security Council of the UN, where, of course, we have a veto. In effect, the United States argued that only it could judge whether its actions were aggression or self-defense. Having so argued, our subsequent insistence that other, smaller states—states without a veto in the Security Council—must submit to the bar of collective judgment looks self-serving rather than principled. Private Judgment—whether manifested in the person of a terrorist like Osama bin Laden or in the agency of a rogue state like Iraq—increasingly reveals itself for the hazard it is. Our own interests as well as our principles demand that we put a stake through its heart. We must not claim it as our special prerogative.

Innocence Revisited

Suppose that the ideas of due process and noncombatant immunity referred to by Carlin Romano are nothing but conventions accepted within and among states. Still, they are precious ideas, hard-won in their application. They require that legitimate institutions resort to violence in ways that discriminate between those adjudicated guilty and those not, between those taking part in hostilities and those not. These are the rules fallible humans have fashioned to keep us out of the State of Nature. They issue, in part, from our collective recognition that the partiality toward our own interests and the unconcern we feel for the interests of others—those two facets of human nature remarked on by Locke—invariably distort Private Judgment and make it unreliable.

But what if you were assured of reliable judgment? What if you were assured of infallibility? Then you would need no conventions of innocence to guide you. No conventional limitations withstand the conceit that God is on your side, since whatever God does must be right. If God orders you to war against, and to "save alive nothing that breatheth" among, an enemy; if He commands you utterly to

destroy the Hittites and the Amorites, the Canaanites and the
Perizzites, the Hivites and the Jebusites; then you destroy without
compunction and without distinction.

When Christians, who from the Middle Ages on have developed
a profoundly influential doctrine of just war that puts special
emphasis on noncombatant immunity and on the innocence, particularly, of those too young, too old, and too ill to be "taking part in
hostilities"—when Christians, I say, read Deuteronomy 20, they
must feel a considerable indigestion. Still, the text says what it says,
and if "God by revelation made the Israelites . . . the executioners of
His supernatural sentence" then the "penalty was within God's
right to assign, and within the Israelites' communicated right to
enforce"—so reads a passage from the *Catholic Encyclopedia*. As
"Sovereign Arbiter of life and death," God can take or give as he
pleases, and it must be just. But we who are without God's eyes
"cannot argue natural right" from these Biblical cases of wholesale
slaughter, the *Encyclopedia* passage goes on to say. Indeed we cannot.
We must hew to those distinctions and discriminations embedded in
the conventions on war and terrorism and we must wholeheartedly
strive to see them everywhere honored.

The delusion that he and God act in concert is what makes Osama
bin Laden's self-election as avenging angel a special threat to humanity. Had he the power, he would not hesitate to kill all that breathes
among his "enemy." He would not hesitate to destroy whole cities,
entire populations. America was "hit by God," declares bin Laden in
his taped message after the September 11 attacks. God has made
America the enemy and bin Laden merely executes His will.

Two days after the September 11 horrors, an unnerved Jerry
Falwell intemperately offered his own version of bin Laden's delir-
ium. God, announced Falwell, had lifted the curtain of protection
around America, angered by the ACLU, gays and lesbians, abortionists, pagans, secularists, and the Federal court system. "God will not
be mocked," he declared. But Falwell quickly repudiated his remarks
in the face of widespread criticism. He apologized for his words,
pleading weariness for his thoughtlessness. "[My] September 13
comments were a complete misstatement of what I believe and what
I've preached for nearly 50 years," Falwell said in an interview.
"Namely, I do not believe that any mortal person knows when God
is judging or not judging someone or a nation." He repeated the
point: "I have no way of knowing when or if God would lift the cur-

tain of protection" around America. "My misstatement included assuming that I or any mortal would know when God is judging or not judging a nation."

In his recantation, Falwell is surely on the mark. He does not know God's will or God's plan. Neither he, nor you, nor I know, nor does Osama bin Laden.

In limning the salutary effects of a little political violence, Thomas Jefferson posed a standard against which to reckon its justification. "What signify a few lives lost in a century or two?" he asked. He meant: the favorable course of events will let us look back from afar and tolerate the violence that set it in motion. If this is the right standard, then the United States has it within its power now, by prudent and measured action, to make sure that in a century or two the lives lost on September 11 continue to signify something—a profound and everlasting wrong.

Sources

Carlin Romano's comments occur in "Why Innocence Matters," *Chronicle of Higher Education*, 48 (October 12, 2001). The texts of the Nuremberg Laws, the Geneva Convention of 1949, and the 1968 United Nations Resolution on Human Rights can be found at www.dannen.com/decision/int-law.html. The UN Convention on the Suppression of Terrorist Bombing (A/RES/52/164) along with other pertinent documents such as Measures to Eliminate International Terrorism (1994) (A/RES/49/60), Human Rights and Terror (1997) (A/RES/52/133/), and Universal Realization of the Right of Peoples to Self-Determination (1997) (A/RES/52/113) can be found at www.un.org/documents/resga.htm. The statement of the League of Arab States and its 1998 Convention on the Suppression of Terrorism are available at www.leagueofarab-states.org/e_LASToday.asp. Judith Lichtenberg, "The Ethics of Retaliation," *Philosophy & Public Policy Quarterly*, vol. 21, no. 4. The characterization of terrorists as a throwback to prehistoric times is by Benzion Netanyahu, "Terrorists and Freedom Fighters," in *Terrorism: How the West Can Win*, edited by Benjamin Netanyahu (Farrar, Straus, Giroux, 1986). Osama bin Laden's statement can be found in the *Washington Post* (October 28, 2001). For the inconveniences in the State of Nature, see Thomas Hobbes, *Leviathan*, edited by Richard Tuck (Cambridge University Press, 1996), Chapters 13, 15, & 29, and John Locke, *Two Treatises of Government* (Mentor Books, 1965), Book II, Chapters 2 and 9. For Jefferson's letters, see Thomas Jefferson, *Writings* (The Library of America, 1984), pp. 881, 889, 911. For the life of John Brown, see Stephen B. Oates, *To Purge This Land with Blood: A Biography of John Brown* (Harper & Row, 1970). My discussion of the Kellogg-Briand Pact draws upon Paul W. Kahn, "From Nuremberg to the Hague: The United States Position in Nicaragua v. United States and the Development of International Law," 12 *Yale Journal of International Law*, vol. 1 (1987). The gloss on Deuteronomy 20 is taken from the 1913 edition of the *Catholic Encyclopedia*, accessible on the Web at www.newadvent.org/cathen/. Jerry Falwell's remarks can be found in Peter Carlson, "Jerry Falwell's Awkward Apology," *Washington Post* (November 18, 2001). A few paragraphs in the text above are taken from R. Fullinwider, "Understanding Terrorism," in *Problems of International Justice*, edited by Steven Luper-Foy (Westview Press, 1988), pp. 248–259 (used by permission).

The Moral Hazards of
Military Response

II

The Paradox of Riskless Warfare

Paul W. Kahn

The fundamental moral fact about war is that the innocent are appropriate targets of physical violence—not, of course, *all* of the morally innocent. The morality of the battlefield distinguishes not between the innocent and the guilty, but between the *combatant* and the *noncombatant*. Combatants, however, cannot be equated with the morally guilty, since opposing combatants are likely to have equally valid claims to moral innocence. Neither has wronged the other, or anyone else. But each *is* licensed, legally and morally, to try to injure or kill the other. Each possesses this license because each acts in self-defense vis-à-vis the other. The reciprocal imposition of risk creates the space that allows injury to the morally innocent. Yet, every military force also has a compelling ethical obligation to minimize the risk of injury to its own forces. Each strives to create an asymmetrical situation in which the enemy suffers the risk of injury while its own forces remain safe. The paradox of riskless warfare arises when the pursuit of asymmetry undermines reciprocity. Without reciprocal imposition of risk, what is the moral basis for injuring the morally innocent?

In this essay, I argue that riskless warfare, which increasingly characterizes US military policy, pushes up against the limits of the traditional moral justification of combat. If it passes those limits, as it arguably did in Kosovo, warfare must become policing. Policing is the application of force to the morally guilty. The moral difference between policing and warfare requires not just different rules of engagement but also different institutions to control the decision to use force. A national army is not, and cannot be, an international police force. Effective international policing requires a credible separation of the application of force from national political interests. A failure to adjust military institutions to the moral grounds of combat will likely result in increasing attacks on our own civilian population.

The Moral Character of Combatants

1. Lack of autonomy. War in the modern age has been fought largely by conscript armies. Conscription makes vivid the contemporary ethical context of soldiering: combatants typically take up the military burden because they have to. That compulsion is likely to rest on physical, political, and legal considerations. The soldier's ethos uses the language of political patriotism, of doing one's duty, of obeying the law, and—most importantly—of confronting uncontrollable circumstance. The combatant's primary concern is the survival of himself and his friends. An ethical demand of independent choice is placed on soldiers only when they have some control: they are not personally to commit war crimes.

Combatants are constrained by forces and circumstances that determine what they "must" do. They tend to be young, with little opportunity to develop an educated opinion. Belief in the justice of their cause is likely to be shaped by propaganda, not deliberation. In some cases—certainly in the case of child soldiers—the combatant is yet another victim of the regime in power, rather than a participant in that regime. Combatants are placed in a situation of mortal danger by political decisions over which they have little, if any, control and which they may not even understand. The only alternative to a combatant's own injury or death may be the successful injuring of another—one who is equally likely to be morally innocent. The morality of contemporary combat emphasizes the mutual moral degradation of combatants: they are not free agents. The role-morality of the combatant begins from a recognition of the suspension of the individual's free choice.

2. The separation of political ends from the morality of combat. Since combatants cannot ordinarily remove themselves from combat because of a moral disagreement with the ends for which they are deployed, their moral status is not the same as that of the political leadership. A combatant who complies with the rules of warfare has not done anything for which he deserves punishment, regardless of which side he fights on. Thus, we didn't think that every German soldier committed a moral wrong for which he deserved to be punished at the end of World War II, even though we thought criminal punishment appropriate for the leadership. We didn't think that the soldiers of the Soviet Union shared in the moral guilt we attributed to much of the political leadership. This is a kind of implicit bargain the state strikes with the individual.

The terms "guilt" and "innocence" don't lose all sense on the battlefield. Rather, they refer to a separate moral code that specifies war crimes. After all, the fundamental reality of the battlefield is a kind of license to kill. That which is prohibited in ordinary life is the point from which moral deliberation begins on the battlefield. Nevertheless, the separation of the political ends of warfare from the morality of combat is always tenuous. The more we believe to be at stake in the outcome of a war, the less willing we are to maintain this distinction. If we thought, for example, that loss of the war would mean the slaughter of all the society's males, and the selling off of the women and children into slavery—the consequences of loss in classical times—we would not be willing to respect the distinction of *jus ad bellum* (principles concerning the just resort to war) from *jus in bello* (principles of just conduct in war). Moderation in political ends is a necessary condition of maintaining the distinct morality of the battlefield.

3. The requirement of reciprocity. The right of combatants to injure and kill each other is founded neither on judgments of their own moral guilt nor on judgments of the moral evil of the end for the sake of which their force is deployed. Rather, combatants are allowed to injure each other just as long as they stand in a relationship of mutual risk. The soldier who takes himself out of combat is no longer a legitimate target. The morality of the battlefield, accordingly, is a variation on the morality of individual self-defense. Injury beyond the point required for self-defense is disproportionate and, therefore, prohibited. Defending himself, the combatant advances the political objective for which force is deployed.

The soldier's privilege of self-defense is subject to a condition of reciprocity. Soldiers cannot defend themselves by threatening to injure noncombatants; they are not permitted civilian reprisals. Combatants cannot threaten the family of an enemy soldier, even if the threat would effectively induce surrender, and thus reduce the overall injuries caused by combat.

These limits do not distinguish the morally guilty from the morally innocent. All may be morally innocent; all are in a tragic and dangerous situation. Nor do such limits necessarily minimize the overall suffering in a war. On efficiency grounds alone, we can never dispose of the claim that ruthlessness in the pursuit of war is the most humane method of fighting, for it brings combat to a swift end. Surely we cannot look at the battlefields of the twentieth century and conclude that the morality of *jus in bello*—just conduct in war—has made wars less costly or more humane.

The rule of reciprocal self-defense cannot be justified by appeal to any of our ordinary moral intuitions: it fails the test of utility, and it also fails the test of deontological rules, since it does not support the moral autonomy and dignity of the individual. Rather, *the rule of reciprocal self-defense stands as its own first principle within a circumscribed context in which individuals act in politically compelled roles.*

If the fundamental principle of the morality of warfare is a right to exercise self-defense within the conditions of mutual imposition of risk, then the emergence of asymmetrical warfare represents a deep challenge. A regime capable of targeting and destroying others with the push of a button, with no human intervention but only the operation of the ultimate high-tech weapon, propels us well beyond the ethics of warfare. Such a deployment of force might be morally justified—it might be used to promote morally appropriate ends—but we cannot appeal to the morality of warfare to justify this mode of combat.

It would be a mistake to believe that we remain sufficiently far from this high-tech image that the problem does not press upon us practically. Riskless warfare can be a product of technological innovation, but it is also a function of political decisions. In Kosovo, Western forces were reported to be operating under a policy that missions were not to be undertaken if there was a serious risk of casualties. The situation in Afghanistan is less clear. While the losses are few, an outsider at least has the impression of reciprocal risk. The political leadership took a different position from that in Kosovo, warning the public that in this case there would be casualties, that sacrifice would be required. There are, however, likely to be more, not fewer, Kosovos in our future.

Asymmetrical Warfare as Police Action

In a previous essay, I identified a number of problems with riskless warfare. It is an image of warfare without the possibility of chivalry. In situations of humanitarian intervention, it expresses a disturbing inequality in the calculus by which we value different lives. It may take the destructive power of war outside of the boundaries of democratic legitimacy, because we are far more willing to delegate the power to use force without risk to the president than we are a power to commit the nation to the sacrifice of its citizens. It is likely to create international accusations of hypocrisy as we choose to intervene in some conflicts and not others, when all are equally a matter of money spent, not lives lost.

All of these are real practical and political problems, but they do not get to the heart of the moral conundrum. At the heart is a violation of the fundamental principle that establishes the internal morality of warfare: self-defense within conditions of reciprocal imposition of risk. Without the imposition of mutual risk, warfare is not war at all. What is it then? It most resembles police enforcement. The moral condition of policing, however, is that only the morally guilty should suffer physical injury. There may be exceptions to this rule, but there is no wholesale license to target the morally innocent.

The ethos of international policing is the same as that of ordinary criminal law enforcement. Individuals are the targets of police actions because of what they have done, not because of who they are. It is no longer enough to know that someone wears a military uniform to make him an appropriate target. Wearing a uniform is not the same as participation in a criminal conspiracy. It is no longer enough to act within the limits of proportionality; we need to protect the morally innocent. We can no longer speak of acceptable collateral damage; we need to obtain a strict correspondence between injury and guilt. If our high-tech weapons, imagined or real, are not limited in their use to the destruction of the morally guilty, then asymmetrical applications of force may satisfy neither the conditions of warfare nor those of policing.

While one can demand of the police that they assume risks in order to protect the morally innocent, there is no moral demand upon the police of symmetrical risk: policing is better to the degree that the police can accomplish their ends without risk to themselves. A perfect technology of justice would achieve a perfect asymmetry: the morally guilty should suffer all the risk and all the injury. This would simultaneously be the ideal technology of policing and the end of warfare.

The motivation to convert traditional political conflicts into matters of law enforcement has not been driven only by the revolution in military technology. The introduction of juridical elements into international relations is one of the great movements of the late twentieth century, ranging across the new activism of the International Court of Justice, the ad hoc tribunals for the former Yugoslavia and Rwanda, and the emerging International Criminal Court. The more we think of international politics under the paradigm of criminal law, the more likely we are to think of the use of force under the paradigm of policing, including its preference for asymmetry. In this sense, asymmetrical warfare represents a sort of moral category confusion.

I don't mean to suggest that there is anything wrong with the movement from warfare to policing. Morally, this can only be seen as progress. The problem is the confusion of the traditional morality of the battlefield with the appropriate morality for contemporary, international policing. If the military is engaged in policing, then it needs to rethink its rules of engagement. When a criminal seizes a hostage, we don't destroy the house in which both are occupants. At least, we don't do so unless we believe there is a virtual certainty that the criminal will injure or kill others if we fail to act immediately. Even then, we demand that every effort be made to protect the innocent hostage. But in many nations, conscripts are little more than hostages—morally speaking—of criminal regimes. We can fight them if we must, but we do not have a license to injure them because of someone else's (or some regime's) wrongdoing. If we cannot adequately discriminate between the morally guilty and the innocent, we may not be able to use force at all. To be sure, many other options remain open: e.g., sanctions, political and financial support of various interests, boycotts, and the pressure of world opinion.

Asymmetry and the Distinction between Combatants and Noncombatants

So far I have argued that, absent the reciprocal imposition of risk, there is no warrant for attacking the morally innocent. To make this argument, I explored the source of the soldier's license to kill, but one can reach this same conclusion by beginning the inquiry from the perspective of the victim. What makes the enemy combatant a morally appropriate *target* for the application of force?

In situations of extreme asymmetry, the distinction between combatants and noncombatants loses its value for moral discrimination. This distinction is central to the ethics of warfare not because it separates the morally guilty from the innocent but because it delineates a domain of threat. If combatants are no longer a threat, however, then they are no more appropriate targets than noncombatants. Both may be the victims of a repressive regime. To identify combatants as appropriate targets under these circumstances is not morally different from identifying the winners of a macabre lottery as the appropriate targets.

To see this point more clearly, suppose that the United States decides that Saddam Hussein's regime is an appropriate target for the use of force. If American forces confront Iraqi forces on a battlefield, then the Iraqi forces are appropriate targets as long as they threaten injury. But if the American forces never show up, what makes these Iraqis appropriate targets? They pose no risk to the United States, and many, if not most, have not done anything wrong. To answer that they provide internal support for the regime does not distinguish Hussein's military forces from many other groups he needs to maintain power. Why not target his bankers or his oil resources? To insist that his army remains an appropriate target, one cannot rely on the ethics of warfare. We need a different set of moral principles that delineates the appropriate targets for what we might, in classic fashion, call uses of force "short of war."

There are three possible responses to this argument. First, combatants are appropriate targets because ultimately *they have consented* to their position, which is one of threatening to use force in support of the regime. Second, although there may not be moral grounds for distinguishing combatants from others, *prudential arguments* support the distinction. Third, although combatants may not threaten an asymmetrically powerful intervener, they nevertheless *threaten others* whom we are entitled to use force to protect. I will treat these arguments in turn.

1. Are combatants appropriate targets because they have consented to their position? As many narratives from Afghanistan are beginning to reveal, it is unrealistic to believe that a morally robust idea of consent operates within authoritarian societies. These are stories of men rounded up and sent to the front, often with little training and rarely with any choice. More important, to rely on consent to identify the legitimate targets for harm is an unjustifiable attempt to extend the moral guilt of the political leadership to the ordinary combatant. If consent is the ground for distinguishing legitimate from illegitimate targets, it is because consent represents a kind of active support of, or participation in, the regime's moral guilt. The regime's active supporters and beneficiaries, however, are not likely to correspond to the traditional category of combatants.

Of course, destroying a regime's army may be a way of destabilizing a regime, but so is destroying elements of its civilian infrastructure or any other significant group of its population. It is no longer the ethics of warfare that legitimates the choice of these targets but the moral value of the end in view.

2. Are these prudential grounds for maintaining the distinction between combatants and others? My arguments so far have proceeded from first principles. For both individuals and nations, however, prudence may sometimes require less principled behavior. Nevertheless, much the same conclusion can be reached from an argument that explores the practical consequences of the application of riskless force.

One consequence of an asymmetrical capacity to apply force can be a self-imposed effort strictly to adhere to the legal limits on targets. Those limits can function as a source of self-constraint. They can also offer an invitation to escalation in the face of frustration, as we saw with the steady expansion of targets in the Kosovo campaign. The list of legal targets can be very long. Scrupulous adherence to lawful targets by an asymmetric power is unlikely to support a perception of legitimacy. In the absence of reciprocal risk, what had traditionally been seen as fair is likely to be seen as morally arbitrary and, if arbitrary, then an act of victimization of the powerless.

Further, conditions of asymmetry are unstable because they compel innovation by the disadvantaged side. Military tactics can be changed in hopes of neutralizing the advantage; for example, guerrilla warfare is one response to technological advantage. Equally possible is the infliction of reciprocal injury on a morally innocent, civilian population. Asymmetry may become an invitation to popular resistance and to terrorism. It is no accident that Saddam Hussein has been developing weapons of mass destruction since his defeat in the Gulf War. His strategy is to create symmetrical risk. If he cannot do this on the battlefield, he will do it elsewhere. The same motivations are powering the Intifada. If the Palestinians cannot hope realistically to create a reciprocal risk for the Israeli military, they will direct the risk of injury at civilians. And, of course, the character of the attack on September 11 was itself a response to the asymmetry in conventional forces. For the asymmetrically powerful to insist on the maintenance of the combatant/noncombatant distinction has the appearance of self-serving moralizing.

Just as it is practically intolerable to suffer an asymmetrical use of force, it is intolerable to suffer an asymmetrical risk to a civilian population. There is likely to be a cycle of escalation, as each side responds to the other's infliction of risk upon noncombatants. The bombing of London was followed by the bombing of Berlin. If it became clear, for example, that Iraq was responsible for the release of anthrax in this country, would the American response respect the line separating combatants from noncombatants? The Israelis allegedly threatened Iraq with just such a retaliation when they perceived a threat of attack by chemical weapons during the Gulf War. It is hard to believe that any country would act differently.

This means that the asymmetrical capacities of Western—and particularly US forces—themselves create the conditions for increasing use of terrorism. This, in turn, creates a cycle of destruction outside of the boundaries of the battlefield, with its reliance on the distinction of combatants from noncombatants.

There is no easy, practical answer to this problem. Military forces cannot be asked to assume unnecessary risks. Every army wants to fight in such a way as to impose a maximum threat to the enemy and a minimum threat to itself. Indeed, it would be immoral for the military leadership not to try to minimize the risk of injury to its own forces. That the moral grounds of warfare may shift at the point at which this ideal approaches reality is not an obvious matter of concern for the internal process of military deliberation. Breaking the cycle requires a transition from combat to policing. There must be a general perception that force is used only against the morally guilty and there must be agreement on who are the morally guilty. This is why contemporary deployments of force tend to end with public, criminal trials.

In both its classical and colonialist forms, asymmetrical power has brought with it an ambition for empire. The capacity to realize ends through the application of force without suffering the risk of reciprocal injury is simultaneously a tactical prize and an intolerable political situation. No state will trust other states with this power. Equally, no people should trust their political leadership with this power. The pursuit of national interests through military means is restrained by the expectation of loss. If that expectation disappears, what are the sources of constraint? Even when legitimate objectives are pursued, the fact that they are the political project of a hegemonic power delegitimizes the application of force in the eyes of both those who suffer the intervention and those who are not directly involved. Riskless warfare may be a prescription for short-term success and long-term disaster.

Riskless warfare will be perceived as hegemonic interference unless it is perceived as legitimate policing. But the latter perception depends on institutional developments. Good intentions are not enough. Human rights claims will be seen as only a form of neocolonialism if advanced through a national military with the capacity risklessly to deploy force. Yet we are only just beginning to develop institutions of international law that could imaginably have a power of policing. Until we do so, we are likely to remain in this paradoxical situation in which the military's capacity for riskless application of force makes our own lives substantially riskier.

3. Does the combatants' threat to others distinguish them from noncombatants? While the United States may be able to use force without risk, others—on the ground—are likely to suffer injuries from the combatants against whom we are intervening. Future uses of force are likely to look like interventions in situations of gross violations of human rights. Those violations constitute the moral ground of the combatants' traditional right to deploy force.

This argument suggests that the moral issue here is not different in kind from traditional arguments of "collective self-defense" when one party aids another in a military conflict. It is morally appropriate for one state to come to the aid of another that has suffered an armed attack. Morally, and increasingly legally, the same rule applies when a people has been attacked by its own government. Typically, interventions in the past have involved supply of material resources—particularly weapons. The deployment of asymmetrical force is simply another variation on this sort of aid. Intervention is morally justifiable so long as the side on whose behalf one intervenes faces a reciprocal risk from the target. The recipient of aid is the principal; the state that intervenes is only the agent.

This argument, while powerful, suggests real limits on intervention. First, the asymmetrical application of force morally *depends on a prior and continuing symmetrical application of force.* To target the morally innocent requires an argument of self-defense by those with whom the asymmetric power chooses to ally itself. Second, *the conflict that grounds the intervention must have its own integrity.* It cannot simply be a situation constructed by Western interests—or even by local parties—to create subsequent grounds for an asymmetrical intervention. Third, *asymmetric intervention places considerable pressure on arguments concerning the just resort to war* because the moral grounds for intervention receive no support from any internal dynamic of combatant self-defense.

When the United States chooses intervention, it assumes the moral obligation to make the *right* choice. "Right," here, means more than "supportive of our own political interests." Why and when does the United States have a right to decide the outcome of other peoples' wars? In situations of genuine political dispute, a potential intervener has no such right.

While riskless intervention in support of the victims of gross violations of fundamental human rights is permissible as a form of collective self-defense, this argument is not independent of the sorts of claims considered in the last section. There remains the problem of external perception: why should the rest of the world see intervention by US forces as anything other than a political decision to dictate who will be the winner in a local conflict? Intervention is perceived as neocolonialism in support of that group most likely to advance Western interests. Such perceptions extend the risk to our own civilian population. Internationalization of decisions to use force, within increasingly juridified institutions, is the only possible response to this perception.

Conclusion

My argument can be represented with a highly simplified example. Imagine a confrontation between a champion heavyweight and an untrained lightweight. Suppose the heavyweight proposes that the way to solve their disagreements is to have a fight within the traditional rules of the ring. Because of the asymmetry, most people would find this proposal self-serving rather than fair. Now suppose that the lightweight challenges another lightweight. To this, the heavyweight responds by demanding cessation of the challenge, and he backs that demand with a threat of his own intervention. We would not necessarily object to this form of intervention, but we would ask whether the heavyweight is intervening on the *right* side. If the dispute between the two lightweights is genuine, why should the side against whom intervention is threatened agree that this is an appropriate way to end the dispute? From his point of view, we are just back at the first situation of asymmetrical force.

This example suggests that a shift in moral concern occurs in the two situations. In the first case, we question the *asymmetry itself,* while in the second, we question *the uses for which* force is being deployed. Our intuitions about a "fair fight" carry weight independently of our intuitions about the purpose for which force is deployed. But the stylized account also suggests that these two perspectives cannot remain separate: asymmetry places a particular burden on any decision to use force. As the asymmetry increases, so does our need to find the grounds for a common belief in the legitimacy of the deployment.

Viewed abstractly, this example is precisely the Hobbesian story of the origin of the state: there is a need to concede a monopoly on the legitimate use of force to a single heavyweight, who then retains the responsibility, as well as the capacity, to resolve private disputes. In the international arenas, the United States increasingly finds itself with monopoly power. The problem of practical ethics lies in the difference between these two situations: the United States is the heavyweight, but it does not have the legitimacy of the sovereign.

This essay is based on a paper originally delivered at the US Army War College's Annual Strategy Conference, April 10–11, 2002. The author thanks the participants for their helpful comments.

Sources

At the end of World War II, only twenty-two high-level Nazi officials were indicted at Nuremberg for planning a war of aggression, crimes against humanity and war crimes. Outside of Nuremberg, about 5,000 German soldiers were charged with particular war crimes. Readers interested in the content of the combatants' moral obligations under contemporary humanitarian law should refer to the Statute of the International Criminal Court, Art. 6–8. Concerning the point that the soldier who removes himself from combat is no longer a legitimate target, see Hague Convention IV (1907), Annex of Regulations, Art. 23; Statute of the International Criminal Court, Art. 8, sec. 2(b)(vi). My earlier discussion of some problems of riskless warfare can be found in Paul W. Kahn, "War and Sacrifice in Kosovo," *Report from the Institute for Philosophy and*

Public Policy, vol. 19, no. 2/3 (Spring/Summer 1999). On the expansion of the target list during the air war in Kosovo, see Michael Ignatieff, *Virtual War: Kosovo and Beyond* (Chatto & Windus, 2001). That we might have reason to worry about the moral integrity of an intervention in Iraq is suggested by recent talk of "creating" a Northern-Alliance type operation in Iraq as a predicate to US action. See, e.g., Inter Press Service, Dec. 2, 2001, "Iraq Veers Back into Washington's Crosshairs," by Jim Lobe, *The Independent* (London), April 8, 2002, (quoting Tony Blair).

The War on Terrorism and the End of Human Rights

David Luban

In the immediate aftermath of September 11, President Bush stated that the perpetrators of the deed would be brought to justice. Soon afterwards, the President announced that the United States would engage in a war on terrorism. The first of these statements adopts the familiar language of criminal law and criminal justice. It treats the September 11 attacks as horrific crimes—mass murders—and the government's mission as apprehending and punishing the surviving planners and conspirators for their roles in the crimes. The War on Terrorism is a different proposition, however, and a different model of governmental action—not law but war. Most obviously, it dramatically broadens the scope of action, because now terrorists who knew nothing about September 11 have been earmarked as enemies. But that is only the beginning.

The Hybrid War-Law Approach

The model of war offers much freer rein than that of law, and therein lies its appeal in the wake of 9/11. First, in war but not in law it is permissible to use lethal force on enemy troops regardless of their degree of personal involvement with the adversary. The conscripted cook is as legitimate a target as the enemy general. Second, in war but not in law "collateral damage," that is, foreseen but unintended killing of combatants, is permissible. (Police cannot blow up an apartment building full of people because a murderer is inside, but an air force can bomb the building if it contains a military target.) Third, the requirements of evidence and proof are drastically weaker in war than in criminal justice. Soldiers do not need proof beyond a reasonable doubt, or even proof by a preponderance of evidence, that someone is an enemy soldier before firing on him or capturing and imprisoning him. They don't need proof at all, merely plausible intelligence. Thus, the US military remains regretful but unapologetic about its January 2002 attack on the Afghani town of Uruzgan, in which twenty-one innocent civilians were killed, based on faulty intelligence that they were al Qaeda fighters. Fourth, in war one can attack an enemy without concern over whether he has done anything. Legitimate targets are those who in the course of combat *might* harm us, not those who *have* harmed us. No doubt there are other significant differences as well. But the basic point should be clear: given Washington's mandate to eliminate the danger of future 9/11s, so far as humanly possible, the model of war offers important advantages over the model of law.

There are disadvantages as well. Most obviously, in war but not in law, fighting back is a *legitimate* response of the enemy. Second, when nations fight a war, other nations may opt for neutrality. Third, because fighting back is legitimate, in war the enemy soldier deserves special regard once he is rendered harmless through injury or surrender. It is impermissible to punish him for his role in fighting the war. Nor can he be harshly interrogated after he is captured. The Third Geneva Convention provides: "Prisoners of war who refuse to answer [questions] may not be threatened, insulted, or exposed to unpleasant or disadvantageous treatment of any kind." And, when the war concludes, the enemy soldier must be repatriated.

Here, however, Washington has different ideas, designed to eliminate these tactical disadvantages in the traditional war model. Washington regards international terrorism not only as a military adversary, but also as a criminal activity and criminal conspiracy. In the law model, criminals don't get to shoot back, and their acts of violence subject them to legitimate punishment. That is what we see in Washington's prosecution of the War on Terrorism. Captured terrorists may be tried before military or civilian tribunals, and shooting back at Americans, including American troops, is a federal crime (for a statute under which John Walker Lindh was indicted criminalizes anyone regardless of nationality, who "outside the United States attempts to kill, or engages in a conspiracy to kill, a national of the United States" or "engages in physical violence with intent to cause serious bodily injury to a national of the United States; or with the result that serious bodily injury is caused to a national of the United States"). Furthermore, the US may rightly demand that other countries not be neutral about murder and terrorism. Unlike the war model, a nation may insist that those who are not with us in fighting murder and terror are against us, because by not joining our operations they are providing a safe haven for terrorists or their bank accounts. By selectively combining elements of the war model and elements of the law model, Washington is able to maximize its own ability to mobilize lethal force against terrorists while eliminating most traditional rights of a military adversary, as well as the rights of innocent bystanders caught in the crossfire.

A Limbo of Rightlessness

The legal status of al Qaeda suspects imprisoned at the Guantanamo Bay Naval Base in Cuba is emblematic of this hybrid war-law approach to the threat of terrorism. In line with the war model, they lack the usual rights of criminal suspects—the presumption of innocence, the right to a hearing to determine guilt, the opportunity to prove that the authorities have grabbed the wrong man. But, in line with the law model, they are considered *unlawful* combatants. Because they are not uniformed forces, they lack the rights of prisoners of war and are liable to criminal punishment. Initially, the American government declared that the Guantanamo Bay prisoners have no rights under the Geneva Conventions. In the face of international protests, Washington quickly backpedaled and announced that the Guantanamo Bay prisoners would indeed be treated as decently as POWs—but it also made clear that the prisoners have no right to such treatment. Neither criminal suspects nor POWs, neither fish nor fowl, they inhabit a limbo of rightlessness. Secretary of Defense Rumsfeld's assertion that the US may continue to detain them even if they are acquitted by a military tribunal dramatizes the point.

To understand how extraordinary their status is, consider an analogy. Suppose that Washington declares a War on Organized Crime. Troops are dispatched to Sicily, and a number of Mafiosi are seized, brought to Guantanamo Bay, and imprisoned without a hearing for the indefinite future, maybe the rest of their lives. They are accused of no crimes, because their capture is based not on what they have done but on what they might do. After all, to become "made" they took oaths of obedience to the bad guys. Seizing them accords with the war model: they are enemy foot soldiers. But they are foot soldiers out of uniform; they lack a "fixed distinctive emblem," in the words of The Hague Convention. That makes them unlawful combatants, so they lack the rights of POWs. They may object that it is only a unilateral declaration by the American President that has turned them into combatants in the first place—he called it a war, they didn't—and that, since they do not regard themselves as literal foot soldiers it never occurred to them to wear a fixed distinctive emblem. They have a point. It seems too easy for the President to divest anyone in the world of rights and liberty simply by announcing that the US is at war with them and then declaring them unlawful combatants if they resist. But, in the hybrid war-law model, they protest in vain.

Consider another example. In January 2002, US forces in Bosnia seized five Algerians and a Yemeni suspected of al Qaeda connections and took them to Guantanamo Bay. The six had been jailed in Bosnia, but a Bosnian court released them for lack of evidence, and the Bosnian Human Rights Chamber issued an injunction that four of them be allowed to remain in the country pending further legal proceedings. The Human Rights Chamber, ironically, was created under US auspices in the Dayton peace accords, and it was designed specifically to protect against treatment like this. Ruth Wedgwood, a well-known international law scholar at Yale and a member of the Council on Foreign Relations, defended the Bosnian seizure in war-model terms. "I think we would simply argue this was a matter of self-defense. One of the fundamental rules of military law is that you have a right ultimately to act in self-defense. And if these folks were actively plotting to blow up the US embassy, they should be considered combatants and captured as combatants in a war." Notice that Professor Wedgwood argues in terms of what the men seized in Bosnia were *planning to do,* not what they *did;* notice as well that the decision of the Bosnian court that there was insufficient evidence does not matter. These are characteristics of the war model.

More recently, two American citizens alleged to be al Qaeda operatives (Jose Padilla, a.k.a. Abdullah al Muhajir, and Yasser Esam Hamdi) have been held in American military prisons, with no crimes charged, no opportunity to consult counsel, and no hearing. The President described Padilla as "a bad man" who aimed to build a nuclear "dirty" bomb and use it against America; and the Justice Department has classified both men as "enemy combatants" who may be held indefinitely. Yet, as military law expert Gary Solis points out, "Until now, as used by the attorney general, the term 'enemy combatant' appeared nowhere in US criminal law, international law or in the law of war." The phrase comes from the 1942 Supreme Court case *Ex parte Quirin*, but all the Court says there is that "an enemy combatant who without uniform comes secretly through the lines for the purpose of waging war by destruction of life or property" would "not . . . be entitled to the status of prisoner of war, but . . . [they would] be offenders against the law of war subject to trial and punishment by military tribunals." For the Court, in other words, the status of a person as a nonuniformed enemy combatant makes him a criminal rather than a warrior, and determines *where* he is tried (in a military, rather than a civilian, tribunal) but not *whether* he is tried. Far from authorizing open-ended confinement, *Ex parte Quirin* presupposes that criminals are entitled to hearings: without a hearing how can suspects prove that the government made a mistake? *Quirin* embeds the concept of "enemy combatant" firmly in the law model. In the war model, by contrast, POWs may be detained without a hearing until hostilities are over. But POWs were captured in uniform, and only their undoubted identity as enemy soldiers justifies such open-ended custody. Apparently, Hamdi and Padilla will get the worst of both models— open-ended custody with no trial, like POWs, but no certainty beyond the US government's say-so that they really are "bad men." This is the hybrid war-law model. It combines the *Quirin* category of "enemy combatant without uniform," used in the law model to justify a military trial, with the war model's practice of indefinite confinement with no trial at all.

The Case for the Hybrid Approach

Is there any justification for the hybrid war-law model, which so drastically diminishes the rights of the enemy? An argument can be offered along the following lines. In ordinary cases of war among states, enemy soldiers may well be morally and politically innocent. Many of them are conscripts, and those who aren't do not necessarily endorse the state policies they are fighting to defend. But enemy soldiers in the War on Terrorism are, by definition, those who have embarked on a path of terrorism. They are neither morally nor politically innocent.

Their sworn aim—"Death to America!"—is to create more 9/11s. In this respect, they are much more akin to criminal conspirators than to conscript soldiers. Terrorists will fight as soldiers when they must, and metamorphose into mass murderers when they can.

Furthermore, suicide terrorists pose a special, unique danger. Ordinary criminals do not target innocent bystanders. They may be willing to kill them if necessary, but bystanders enjoy at least some measure of security because they are not primary targets. Not so with terrorists, who aim to kill as many innocent people as possible. Likewise, innocent bystanders are protected from ordinary criminals by whatever deterrent force the threat of punishment and the risk of getting killed in the act of committing a crime offer. For a suicide bomber, neither of these threats is a deterrent at all—after all, for the suicide bomber one of the hallmarks of a *successful* operation is that he winds up dead at day's end. Given the unique and heightened danger that suicide terrorists pose, a stronger response that grants potential terrorists fewer rights may be justified. Add to this the danger that terrorists may come to possess weapons of mass destruction, including nuclear devices in suitcases. Under circumstances of such dire menace, it is appropriate to treat terrorists as though they embody the most dangerous aspects of both warriors and criminals. That is the basis of the hybrid war-law model.

The Case against Expediency

The argument against the hybrid war-law model is equally clear. The US has simply chosen the bits of the law model and the bits of the war model that are most convenient for American interests, and ignored the rest. The model abolishes the rights of potential enemies (and their innocent shields) by fiat—not for reasons of moral or legal principle, but solely because the US does not want them to have rights. The more rights they have, the more risk they pose. But Americans' urgent desire to minimize our risks doesn't make other people's rights disappear. Calling our policy a War on Terrorism obscures this point.

The theoretical basis of the objection is that the law model and the war model each comes as a package, with a kind of intellectual integrity. The law model grows out of relationships within states, while the war model arises from relationships between states. The law model imputes a ground-level community of values to those subject to the law—paradigmatically, citizens of a state, but also visitors and foreigners who choose to engage in conduct that affects a state. Only because law imputes shared basic values to the community can a state condemn the conduct of criminals and inflict punishment on them. Criminals deserve condemnation and punishment because their conduct violates norms that we are entitled to count on their sharing. But, for the same reason—the imputed community of values—those subject to the law ordinarily enjoy a presumption of innocence and an expectation of safety. The government cannot simply grab them and confine them without making sure they have broken the law, nor can it condemn them without due process for ensuring that it has the right person, nor can it knowingly place bystanders in mortal peril in the course of fighting crime. They are our fellows, and the community should protect them just as it protects us. The same imputed community of values that justifies condemnation and punishment creates rights to due care and due process.

War is different. War is the ultimate acknowledgment that human beings do not live in a single community with shared norms. If their norms conflict enough, communities pose a physical danger to each other, and nothing can safeguard a community against its enemies except force of arms. That makes enemy soldiers legitimate targets; but it makes our soldiers legitimate targets as well, and, once the enemy no longer poses a danger, he should be immune from punishment, because if he has fought cleanly he has violated no norms that we are entitled to presume he honors. Our norms are, after all, *our* norms, not his.

Because the law model and war model come as conceptual packages, it is unprincipled to wrench them apart and recombine them simply because it is in America's interest to do so. To declare that Americans can fight enemies with the latitude of warriors, but if the enemies fight back they are not warriors but criminals, amounts to a kind of heads-I-win-tails-you-lose international morality in which whatever it takes to reduce American risk, no matter what the cost to others, turns out to be justified. This, in brief, is the criticism of the hybrid war-law model.

To be sure, the law model could be made to incorporate the war model merely by rewriting a handful of statutes. Congress could enact laws permitting imprisonment or execution of persons who pose a significant threat of terrorism whether or not they have already done anything wrong. The standard of evidence could be set low and the requirement of a hearing eliminated. Finally, Congress could authorize the use of lethal force against terrorists regardless of the danger to innocent bystanders, and it could immunize officials from lawsuits or prosecution by victims of collateral damage. Such statutes would violate the Constitution, but the Constitution could be amended to incorporate antiterrorist exceptions to the Fourth, Fifth, and Sixth Amendments. In the end, we would have a system of law that includes all the essential features of the war model.

It would, however, be a system that imprisons people for their intentions rather than their actions, and that offers the innocent few protections against mistaken detention or inadvertent death through collateral damage. Gone are the principles that people should never be punished for their thoughts, only for their deeds, and that innocent people must be protected rather than injured by their own government. In that sense, at any rate, repackaging war as law seems merely cosmetic, because it replaces the ideal of law as a protector of rights with the more problematic goal of protecting some innocent people by sacrificing others. The hypothetical legislation incorporates war into law only by making law as partisan and ruthless as war. It no longer resembles law as Americans generally understand it.

The Threat to International Human Rights

In the War on Terrorism, what becomes of international human rights? It seems beyond dispute that the war model poses a threat to international human rights, because honoring human rights is neither practically possible nor theoretically required during war. Combatants are legitimate targets; noncombatants maimed by accident or mistake are regarded as collateral damage rather than victims of atrocities; cases of mistaken identity get killed or confined without a hearing because combat conditions preclude due process. To be sure, the laws of war specify minimum human rights, but these are far less robust than rights in peacetime—and the hybrid war-law model reduces this schedule of rights even further by classifying the enemy as unlawful combatants.

One striking example of the erosion of human rights is tolerance of torture. It should be recalled that a 1995 al Qaeda plot to bomb eleven US airliners was thwarted by information tortured out of a Pakistani suspect by the Philippine police—an eerie real-life version of the familiar philosophical thought-experiment. The *Washington Post* reports that since September 11 the US has engaged in the summary transfer of dozens of terrorism suspects to countries where they will be interrogated under torture. But it isn't just the United States that has proven willing to tolerate torture for security reasons. Last December, the Swedish government snatched a suspected Islamic extremist to whom it had previously granted political asylum, and the same day had him transferred to Egypt, where Amnesty International reports that he has been tortured to the point where he walks only with difficulty. Sweden is not, to say the least, a traditionally hard-line nation on human rights issues. None of this international transportation is lawful—indeed, it violates international treaty obligations under the Convention against Torture that in the US have constitutional status as "supreme Law of the Land"—but that may not matter under the war model, in which even constitutional rights may be abrogated.

It is natural to suggest that this suspension of human rights is an exceptional emergency measure to deal with an unprecedented threat. This raises the question of how long human rights will remain suspended. When will the war be over?

Here, the chief problem is that the War on Terrorism is not like any other kind of war. The enemy, Terrorism, is not a territorial state or nation or government. There is no opposite number to negotiate with. There is no one on the other side to call a truce or declare a ceasefire, no one among the enemy authorized to surrender. In traditional wars among states, the war aim is, as Clausewitz argued, to impose one state's political will on another's. The *aim* of the war is not to kill the enemy—killing the enemy is the *means* used to achieve the real end, which is to force capitulation. In the War on Terrorism, no capitulation is possible. That means that the real aim of the war is, quite simply, to kill or capture all of the terrorists—to keep on killing and killing, capturing and capturing, until they are all gone.

Of course, no one expects that terrorism will ever disappear completely. Everyone understands that new anti-American extremists, new terrorists, will always arise and always be available for recruitment and deployment. Everyone understands that even if al Qaeda is destroyed or decapitated, other groups, with other leaders, will arise in its place. It follows, then, that the War on Terrorism will be a war that can only be abandoned, never concluded. The War has no natural resting point, no moment of victory or finality. It requires a mission of killing and capturing, in territories all over the globe, that will go on in perpetuity. It follows as well that the suspension of human rights implicit in the hybrid war-law model is not temporary but permanent.

Perhaps with this fear in mind, Congressional authorization of President Bush's military campaign limits its scope to those responsible for September 11 and their sponsors. But the War on Terrorism has taken on a life of its own that makes the Congressional authorization little more than a technicality. Because of the threat of nuclear terror, the American leadership actively debates a war on Iraq regardless of whether Iraq was implicated in September 11; and the President's yoking of Iraq, Iran, and North Korea into a single axis of evil because they back terror suggests that the War on Terrorism might eventually encompass all these nations. If the US ever unearths tangible evidence that any of these countries is harboring or abetting terrorists with weapons of mass destruction, there can be little doubt that Congress will support military action. So too, Russia invokes the American War on Terrorism to justify its attacks on Chechen rebels, China uses it to deflect criticisms of its campaign against Uighur separatists, and Israeli Prime Minister Sharon explicitly links military actions against Palestinian insurgents to the American War on Terrorism. No doubt there is political opportunism at work in some or all of these efforts to piggyback onto America's campaign, but the opportunity would not exist if "War on Terrorism" were merely the code name of a discrete, neatly-boxed American operation. Instead, the War on Terrorism has become a model of politics, a worldview with its own distinctive premises and consequences. As I have argued, it includes a new model of state action, the hybrid war-law model, which depresses human rights from their peacetime standard to the war-time standard, and indeed even further. So long as it continues, the War on Terrorism means the end of human rights, at least for those near enough to be touched by the fire of battle.

Sources

On the January 2002 attack on the Afghani town of Uruzgan, see: John Ward Anderson, "Afghans Falsely Held by U.S. Tried to Explain; Fighters Recount Unanswered Pleas, Beatings—and an Apology on Their Release," *Washington Post* (March 26, 2002); see also Susan B. Glasser, "Afghans Live and Die With U.S. Mistakes; Villagers Tell of Over 100 Casualties," *Washington Post* (Feb. 20, 2002). On the Third Geneva Convention, see: Geneva Convention (III) Relative to the Treatment of Prisoners of War, 6 U.S.T. 3317, signed on August 12, 1949, at Geneva, Article 17. Although the US has not ratified the Geneva Convention, it has become part of customary international law, and certainly belongs to the war model. Count One of the Lindh indictment charges him with violating 18 U.S.C. 2332(b), "Whoever outside the United States attempts to kill, or engages in a conspiracy to kill, a national of the United States" may be sentenced to 20 years (for attempts) or life imprisonment (for conspiracies). Subsection (c) likewise criminalizes "engag[ing] in physical violence with intent to cause serious bodily injury to a national of the United States; or with the result that serious bodily injury is caused to a national of the United States." Lawful combatants are defined in the Hague Convention (IV) Respecting the Laws and Customs of War on Land, Annex to the Convention, 1 Bevans 631, signed on October 18, 1907, at The Hague, Article 1. The definition requires that combatants "have a fixed distinctive emblem recognizable at a distance." Protocol I Additional to the Geneva Conventions of 1949, 1125 U.N.T.S. 3, adopted on June 8, 1977, at Geneva, Article 44 (3) makes an important change in the Hague Convention, expanding the definition of combatants to include non-uniformed irregulars. However, the United States has not agreed to Protocol I. The source of Ruth Wedgwood's remarks: Interview with Melissa Block, National Public Radio program, "All Things Considered" (January 18, 2002); Gary Solis, "Even a 'Bad Man' Has Rights," *Washington Post* (June 25, 2002); *Ex parte Quirin*, 317 U.S. 1, 31 (1942). On the torture of the Pakistani militant by Philippine police: Doug Struck et al., "Borderless Network Of Terror; Bin Laden Followers Reach Across Globe," *Washington Post* (September 23, 2001): "'For weeks, agents hit him with a chair and a long piece of wood, forced water into his mouth, and crushed lighted cigarettes into his private parts,' wrote journalists Marites Vitug and Glenda Gloria in *Under the Crescent Moon*, an acclaimed book on Abu Sayyaf. 'His ribs were almost totally broken and his captors were surprised he survived.'" On US and Swedish transfers of Isamic militants to countries employing torture: Rajiv Chandrasakaran & Peter Finn, "U.S. Behind Secret Transfer of Terror Suspects," *Washington Post* (March 11, 2002); Peter Finn, "Europeans Tossing Terror Suspects Out the Door," *Washington Post* (January 29, 2002); Anthony Shadid, "Fighting Terror/Atmosphere in Europe, Military Campaign/Asylum Bids; in Shift, Sweden Extradites Militants to Egypt," *Boston Globe* (December 31, 2001). Article 3(1) of the Convention against Torture provides that "No State Party shall expel, return ('*refouler*') or extradite a person to another State where there are substantial grounds for believing that he would be in danger of being subjected to torture." Article 2(2) cautions that "No exceptional circumstances whatsoever, whether a state of war or a threat of war, internal political instability or any other public emergency, may be invoked as a justification of torture." But no parallel caution is incorporated into Article 3(1)'s non-*refoulement* rule, and a lawyer might well argue that its absence implies that the rule may be abrogated during war or similar public emergency. *Convention against Torture and Other Cruel, Inhuman or Degrading Treatment or Punishment*, 1465 U.N.T.S. 85. Ratified by the United States, Oct. 2, 1994. Entered into force for the United States, Nov. 20, 1994. (Article VI of the US Constitution provides that treaties are the "supreme Law of the Land.")

Looking Ahead:
The Possibility of a
Comprehensive Approach

III

Is Development an Effective Way to Fight Terrorism?

Lloyd J. Dumas

Recently columnist Thomas Friedman and economist Alan B. Kreuger, both writing in the *New York Times,* have argued that development is not an effective tool for fighting terrorism. Many terrorists, the argument goes, are not poor—-certainly not desperately poor—-and many people living in poverty do not become involved in terrorism. But other analysts, such as Richard Sokolsky and Joseph McMillan, research fellows at the Institute for National Strategic Studies of the National Defense University, have argued that development is crucial to countering terrorism. They contend that poverty and the frustration it breeds are key elements in creating the conditions that foster and support terrorism worldwide.

To productively address the issue of the possible relation between terrorism and the need for development, one must understand more clearly the nature of terrorism. One must also distinguish terrorism from both the classic military actions of rebels and ordinary criminal violence. One must also understand the values, conditions, and motivations that lead people to engage in appallingly destructive acts of terrorism.

The Nature of Terrorism

Not every violent, destructive, or antisocial act is terrorism. Terrorism is defined by its tactics and strategy: it is violence or the threat of violence carried out with the express purpose of creating fear and alarm. An armed gang of bank robbers that shoot bank guards commit a violent crime, not an act of terrorism. The robbers' intent in attacking the guards is to prevent the guards from interfering with the theft, not to frighten the wider population. But when a gang randomly plants bombs on city buses, it is not trying to stop the passengers from interfering with its activities; it is trying to frighten people. This is a terrorist gang because the purpose of its acts is to terrorize. Unlike the bank robbers, this gang intends its acts to have effects that, in space and time, reach far beyond the immediate damage they have inflicted.

Unlike other criminals, further, terrorists usually try to draw attention to themselves, often claiming "credit" for their acts. In many ways, terrorism is a perverse form of theater in which terrorists play to an audience whose actions—and opinions—they hope to influence. When terrorists kidnap journalists or tourists, for instance, they play to an audience of government officials who possess the power to grant such typical demands as the release of the terrorists' imprisoned comrades. But even in these cases, the terrorists are playing to the public at the same time, with a view toward creating enough public pressure to compel those in power to do what the terrorists want done.

It is the nature of terrorism to encourage public vulnerability, insecurity, and helplessness. Commonly, choosing victims more or less at random is the best way to accomplish this goal. Randomness works— if there seems no clear pattern regarding *which* particular bus is blown up, airliner hijacked, or building bombed, then there exist no obvious or certain ways for a bystander to avoid becoming a victim, no clear strategy to guard against danger. As a consequence, fear and anxiety grow—and remain a part of life of the average member of the public.

Acts intended to frighten the public, committed against more-or-less randomly chosen victims, who themselves are powerless to meet the attackers' demands, define terrorism and set it apart from other forms of violence. By contrast, bombing the barracks of an occupying military force is not an act of terrorism, but a violent and murderous act of war. Its victims are not randomly chosen innocent bystanders, but those who are *directly* involved in carrying out policies and activities the attackers oppose. Similarly, the act of a habitual sex offender who kidnaps, rapes, and murders a more-or-less randomly chosen victim is a vicious and brutal crime, but it also is not terrorism. Though predatory crimes often instill fear in the public, such crimes are neither committed for that purpose nor intended to influence public opinion or behavior. Suicide bombing an urban marketplace to precipitate a change in government policy is an act of terrorism because, although its more-or-less randomly chosen victims cannot directly change government behavior, the indiscriminate slaughter caused by suicide bombing is intended to shock and frighten people into demanding changes in government policies sought by the terrorists. So long as the public believes that it remains in danger of further random attack until those policies change, it will insist all the more urgently on government action.

Note that this conceptual definition of terrorism as a tactic— committing acts intended to instill public fear, against more-or-less randomly chosen victims who themselves are powerless to meet their attackers' demands—has nothing to do with the ultimate goals of those who choose this tactic. Regardless whether a group is trying to overthrow a democratic government and establish a dictatorship, create a homeland for a disenfranchised people, trigger a race war, or get more food distributed to the malnourished—if it uses terrorist means, it is a terrorist group.

Because terrorism is a *tactic* and not an *end* in itself, as many motivations and goals exist as there are people who might resort to terrorism. At one end of the spectrum are those who are deeply disturbed, mentally and emotionally. The economic and political conditions of such deranged individuals are wholly irrelevant to their desire to commit mayhem. At the other extreme are those motivated by a desire to achieve specific and relatively limited political objectives—such as freeing Northern Ireland from British control, or ending the Israeli occupation of the Palestinian territories. These individuals have chosen terrorism on the basis of a rational, though horrific, calculation (which may or may not be correct) that terrorism will publicize their cause and build enough pressure to help them accomplish their goals.

In arguing against the efficacy of development in fighting terrorism, Alan Kreuger contends that good empirical evidence exists to show that the commission of hate crimes is unrelated to either the education level or economic condition of the perpetrators of those crimes. Since hate crimes are a "close cousin" to terrorism, he argues, education level and economic conditions are irrelevant to the making of a terrorist. It may well be true that the commission of hate crimes bears no significant relation to socioeconomic status, since these crimes tend to be driven by pure bigotry, which is not the private domain of any particular socioeconomic group. But hate crimes are *not* "close cousins" of terrorism. They are not even second cousins twice removed. No doubt hatred fills the hearts of at least some terrorists, but terrorism is an entirely different phenomenon.

The Terrorist Perspective

All but the most insane, most isolated terrorists (such as Ted Kaczynski, the Unabomber) to some extent depend on and try to build support among a broader public, at least for their cause if not for their tactics. Most terrorists lack the benefit of a wealthy patron like Osama bin Laden, or the active support of a state. But even those who do enjoy some form of high-level patronage must still succeed at a variety of practical, and usually expensive tasks. These include recruiting new members, training them, finding methods that enable them to travel, planning and coordinating activities and logistics, and storing matériel and equipment—all without detection. Terrorists are much more likely to successfully accomplish these practical tasks if they can count on a base of support among a wider public.

Although a terrorist group could rely on deranged or financially desperate individuals to meet its recruitment needs, such people are dangerous to the group's discipline, effectiveness, and stability. The group is better served by members possessing financial means and skills, and mental stability. Among other things, a core membership of people who seem more solidly based allows the group to more easily recruit others who themselves have some financial means and are relatively stable psychologically. But the problem then becomes how to motivate such recruits to take extreme—even terminal—risks.

Among the most successful recruitment appeals is the call to the service of some group or force greater than the individuals themselves. This appeal to heroic participation in a greater cause encourages recruits to feel that by engaging in terrorism, the recruit becomes the avenger of some great wrong, the voice of the voiceless, a soldier for the weak and oppressed. Experience has shown that the right kind of appeal to heroic participation in a "great cause" can make recruits not just ready but eager to perpetrate extreme acts of violence against innocent people who have never directly done them any harm.

Those who consider themselves (or their close friends and families) victims of economic and political oppression and marginalization are easiest to recruit to "fight back" against their perceived victimizers. Retaliation can take the form of either direct engagement in terrorism or support of its activities. A wider public that becomes convinced it is part of the oppressed group may condone or support terrorism. For example, it seems not only that the IRA terrorists were less disadvantaged than many other Catholics in Northern Ireland, but also that many of the IRA's financial supporters in the US were also far from destitute. But both the terrorists and their supporters considered themselves fighters against the forces responsible for the economic and political marginalization of "their people."

Similarly, the perpetrators of the September 11 attacks were certainly not themselves either economically disadvantaged or politically oppressed. Most were of the middle class, and they were reasonably well educated. At the same time, they saw themselves as striking a blow for "their oppressed people," their "Muslim brothers" who were forced to bear the insult of "foreign infidels" (American military forces) occupying their holiest of lands of Saudi Arabia and enjoying the support of the powerful Saudi government. The September 11 attackers might also have seen themselves as striking a blow against America as the strong supporter of Israel, "fighting back" on behalf of their "Muslim brothers" in Palestine, who are indisputably in dire straits.

Terrorism, which by definition is always directed against innocent, uninvolved civilians, is never justifiable. Nevertheless, understanding terrorist motivations and worldview does not imply sympathy with either their means or their goals. Instead it is important because it helps to explain why terrorists do what they do. Their attention to and interest in maintaining wider public support, for example, are not just incidental but are critical to both solving their practical problems and encouraging added public pressure to achieve their goals.

Terrorism and Development

The more that inclusive economic *and* political development increase the economic well-being and political status of the wider group of which terrorists and their supporters feel they are a part, the more difficult it becomes for terrorists to recruit operatives and to find others who will support the terrorists' cause. It is in this sense, then, that economic and political development will in the long run help dry up the pool of potential terrorists, as well as the wider public support on which they depend.

To believe that one's people are not respected and that one's views and needs are not taken seriously by the rest of the world are powerful motivations toward violence. But these motivations can be short-circuited by opening political avenues for peaceful dialogue to air grievances and to present views and goals. One possibility is giving terrorists a seat at the political table—but not necessarily a seat at the *head* of the table. Within its own political system, Israel for instance has from time to time brought together politicians advocating vastly disparate views into "national unity" governments. But not every participant in these government coalitions has been influential in a wide range of key policies.

Perhaps a better example is a scene I recall from a 1980s public television documentary about Costa Rica. The documentary included an in-depth look at Costa Rican political attitudes. At one point the North American interviewer, shocked to learn that the communists held about four percent of the seats in the national legislature, said something like, "You've got COMMUNISTS in the legislature!" To which the Costa Rican official he was interviewing said, in effect: "Yes, we do. We decided we'd rather have them in the legislature shouting at us than in the hills shooting at us."

The best way to deal with terrorism that arises from individual mental illness or group psychosis is through first-rate intelligence and police work, not political accommodation or economic development. But terrorism that arises from political and economic marginalization can be more effectively short-circuited by giving voice to a wide array of groups with *genuine* political agendas (not doomsday religious cults or psychopaths). Civil participation dissolves the frustration and marginalization that encourages terrorism or supports it. Political development, which provides avenues for the peaceful participation of groups representing widely diverse interests, is an integral part of an effective counter-terrorist strategy.

One important question to ask is why disenfranchised groups turn to terrorism rather than to more traditional forms of civil rebellion or to guerrilla warfare. Of course, some groups do choose to become rebels or guerillas. Successful rebellion depends in part on the ability to raise large enough forces for direct confrontation with the government. If a disenfranchised group can raise significant forces—and especially if the government is relatively weak—it may tend to form guerrilla groups. If it cannot—and especially if the governmental opposition is likely to be strong—the disenfranchised group might choose terrorism. The group might also turn to terrorism if it viewed its "real" enemy as a foreign government or corporate cabal that is either far beyond its borders, too powerful to confront directly, or both.

Maximizing the Counter-Terrorist Effects of Development

Some approaches to development will be more effective than others in fighting terrorism. I have argued that, regardless of the socioeconomic status of either the terrorists themselves or their financial supporters, the crux of the problem lies in the economic and political marginalization, frustration, and humiliation of the group to which the terrorists and their supporters feel connected. If so, then the approach to development likely to prove most effective against terrorism is one that both reaches out directly to the most marginalized, disaffected, and disadvantaged of those people, and also allows individuals a sense of empowerment, self-worth, dignity, and respect. The most effective program will also be one that simultaneously addresses the challenges of both economic and political development.

On the economic side, I am a strong advocate of microlending. Putting a little capital—and the responsibility for repayment of that capital—in many different impoverished hands helps overcome the barriers created by lack of access to the means of self-investment, as well as the lack of self-confidence and hope. It is also possible, even necessary, to seamlessly incorporate an educational element into microlending programs. One of the most interesting and encouraging examples of the ability of microlending to bring real economic improvement and social empowerment to the poor is the Grameen Bank of Bangladesh.

Founded in 1976 by economist Muhammad Yunus, the Grameen Bank has enabled millions of poor Bangladeshis to start or upgrade their own small businesses. The Grameen Bank makes very small loans—often less than a few hundred dollars—to five-person borrower groups. Most of these loans were made to women, a particularly disadvantaged, economically (and politically) marginalized part of that nation's population. This approach has been impressive in its outreach ability. As impressive is the astonishing loan repayment rate of over 90 percent, achieved by the design of culturally sensitive loan programs that consider the needs of its borrowers. The success of the Grameen approach makes it clear that any microlending program must rely on knowledge of the cultural environment in order to design procedures that assure responsible use of funds and their timely repayment.

On the political side, democratization must extend beyond the mere formalities of holding elections. It must guarantee the right to organize political parties that offer meaningful alternatives. The process of democratization also must protect (and, in some circumstances, establish) the freedom of speech and of the press, and it must allow avenues for peaceful political participation. Greater opportunity for political expression also requires the protection of those whose views lie outside the political mainstream, and the protection of ethnic minorities. Greater opportunity for peaceful participation in political and economic life benefits those who would otherwise be disenfranchised—and also the wider society, which can choose from among a wider pool of ideas and talents of the population.

International organizations as large as the World Bank and the International Monetary Fund can best assist by *not* becoming directly involved in microlending. Such organizations should encourage the establishment and funding of a variety of microlending institutions in developing countries. International organizations can also help assure that both transparency and the inclusion of corrective feedback systems are part of the design and implementation of programs.

In both the economic and political arenas, the creation of institutions that encourage, support, and facilitate the development of nongovernmental organizations (NGOs) can be vital in achievement of the kinds of deep and wide outreach that thwart the allure of terrorism. Care must be taken to assure that these organizations are genuine real grassroots groups and not "Astroturf" NGOs—those that look like grassroots organizations from a distance, but actually represent the interests of influential business or governing elites in the country. If counter-terrorism is to succeed, the voiceless must be given voice. The genuine grassroots NGO will invigorate active participation in political and economic life. Large, government-based organizations dealing with international development (such as a the World Bank or the US Agency for International Development) should not directly involve themselves in the creation of NGOs. NGOs that are born of the efforts of local activists are far more effective at representing local interests and creating a real sense of empowerment. The involvement of international organizations could prove counterproductive if, for instance, their enactment or management of programs is based on a misunderstanding or misrepresentation of local interest. International organizations contribute best when they help fund and encourage the creation of those institutions that provide the substrate on which genuine grassroots NGOs grow and flourish.

Conclusion

Because terrorism is such a violent tactic, because it inflicts so much pain on the innocent, it fills us with anger and the urge to strike back even more violently against those whom we judge have encouraged—let alone committed—such despicable acts. Strong emotional reactions to terrorism are easy enough to understand. But a response based on emotion leads only to more pain, more destruction, more taking of innocent lives. This kind of response is not only profoundly immoral, it is profoundly ineffective.

Anyone who needs proof of the futility of this kind of response as a counter-terrorist strategy should consider the Israeli-Palestinian conflict. For decades, Israel has doggedly followed a policy of responding to any act of terrorism with violent military retaliation. Many have died as a result; yet not only has this policy failed to stop the terrorism, but there exists today more terrorism directed against Israel than ever before. What has this vicious cycle of violence accomplished? Neither side has achieved its objectives. The only result one sees with this policy is the creation of a situation in which Israelis live in fear and Palestinians live in misery—clearly an intolerable life for anyone.

There exist far more effective responses to terrorism and—even more important—more effective efforts to prevent terrorism. In the short run, high-quality intelligence gathering and police work are critical. But in the long run, encouraging economic and political development is the single most effective counter-terrorist approach. Only carefully crafted development programs can fully and directly address terrorism's root causes: the marginalization, frustration, and humiliation that breeds not just terrorism, but also other forms of violence and inhumanity that characterize deprived populations. In the long run, if they follow the right sorts of policies, the institutions of international development will prove to be a far more potent counter-terrorist force in the world than military forces could ever hope to be.

Terrorism is a complex phenomenon. Like other forms of violence, there is no single reason why people engage in acts of terrorism, and no simple solution to the problems it poses. But if we wish to move beyond vengeance and seek a solution, we must try to understand and effectively address the conditions that give rise to terrorism and help it grow. In our search for a solution, there is no doubt that economic and political development play a critical role. They are not the whole answer, but they are an important part of it.

Sources

Thomas Friedman and Alan B. Kreuger expressed their reservations about development as effective in combating terrorism in the "Economic Scene" column of the *New York Times* (December 13, 2001); Richard Sokolsky and Joseph McMillan,"Foreign Aid in Our Own Defense," *New York Times* (February 12, 2002); more information on the Grameen Bank can be found in: Muhammad Yunus with Alan Jolis, *Banker to the Poor: Micro-lending and the Battle Against World Poverty* (Public Affairs, 1999); further thoughts on the nature of terrorism and the threat it poses can be found in: Lloyd J. Dumas: *Lethal Arrogance: Human Fallibility and Dangerous Technologies* (St. Martin's Press/Palgrave, 1999).

The War of All against All:
Terror and the Politics of Fear

Benjamin R. Barber

Terrorism appears in the first instance as an impressive display of brute power, but it is in fact a strategy of fear not force. It arises out of weakness—powerlessness—and succeeds only by turning the power of its stronger adversaries against them. It is a kind of strategic jujitsu that cannot win other than by leveraging others into losing, overcoming them by dint of their own force and their own fear. The diabolical intelligence behind the World Trade Center and Pentagon attacks was evident not so much in the crude but demonically imaginative use of passenger planes as firebombs but in the ensuing manipulation of fear that closed down the air transportation system and the stockmarkets. Bioterror has likewise been effective not as deed (only a handful of deaths) but as a tool of paralysis (whether by domestic or international terrorists is not yet known). By attacking the media, it aroused personal fear in those who shape public opinion, producing a multiplier effect that allowed relatively minor real damage to create maximum havoc.

In binding us to our own fear through what the anarchist Bakunin called the "propaganda of the deed," the terrorists have in a certain sense undone the social contract, bringing us full circle back to a kind of "state of nature." For the last four hundred years, we travelled a road from anarchy, insecurity and fear (the state of nature postulated by social contract theorists like Hobbes and Locke) to law and order (lawful order), political safety and the enjoyment of civil liberty. Operating outside the law, making insecurity ubiquitous and turning liberty into risk, terrorism pushes us backwards into a quasi-anarchy. To understand fully what this means is to enter the world of political philosophy. While there is much that is "new" in our current condition—technology, global interdependence, metastasizing extremisms only loosely related to their justifying ideologies and religions—there is also much that is old: the breakdown of civility and legal order as a consequence of civil strife and war, a sense of sovereignty's inefficacy under pressure of terror and uncertainty; and the usefulness of the metaphor of the "state of nature" in the international sector where civilization's normal "inside-the-state" certainties no longer obtain and where human life, in Hobbe's stark terms, is often violent, nasty, brutish, and short.

The dilemma with which the puzzle of modern terrorism begins is a straightforward consequence of social contract logic: in a democracy, people are not supposed to throw bombs. Democracy means arbitration of conflict by words and votes, not force and violence. Force and fraud, as Thomas Hobbes put it, are the cardinal virtues of the state of nature where there is no law. They are supposed to be superceded by consent and legitimacy under normal social conditions. If in our democracy bombs are still thrown, then either there is something wrong with the bomb-throwers or something amiss with our democracy, something that pushes us back into that very anarchic state of nature from which democratic sovereignty was meant to deliver us.

Now clearly there is a great deal wrong with the terrorists: their actions are predominantly the consequence of pathology and yield neither to rational analysis nor understanding, let alone justification. But there is also something amiss in our democracy, something increasingly problematic about its founding norms of sovereignty and independence. The first problem—pathological terrorism—will be dealt with and (we must hope) disposed of by special military and intelligence operations. But this second problem is my subject here, for its resolution will turn on civic and democratic action and will engage all of us in its business.

Under normal circumstances, there should be no need to use violence, let alone conduct terrorist operations, in a democracy. It is the object of democratic governance to permit participation and voice by "subjects" (who hence become citizens) such that force is quite literally beside the point. Tyranny breeds violence because it represses every other alternative. Violence is not the instrument of choice even under tyrannical governments because confrontations based on force usually favor the powerful—that is, the tyrants. But it can become the choice of those so disempowered by a political order (or a political disorder) that they have no other options. This was the position of Algerian nationalists facing the French in the 1950s and the African National Congress facing South African apartheid in the 1980s, where terrorism became a weapon of resisters.

Democrats are however always confused by terrorists because terrorism is always inexplicable within the democratic frame. Hence the plaintive query of so many Americans after September 11: "Why don't they like us? What did we do wrong?" What becomes quickly apparent is that those who use violence, with or without justification, generally do not share the perception that they have "democratic" options, whether that means "access" to power or the capacity to play a role in shaping the *res publica* (the domain of public things).

We can question the perception and judgment of those who make such arguments about our system, and we can simply dismiss them (deal with them) as lunatics and demons, writing them off as "the evil ones." After all, their deeds are aptly enough described as evil. But we also have to ask whether our democracy as it shapes the global society gives, if not them, those who sympathize with them, the access of which we boast. Terrorists are rarely themselves genuine democrats and they generally use the rhetoric of freedom and oppression to rationalize nihilistic objectives. But the sea of fearful, oppressed, and abused peoples in whom terrorists hope to arouse sympathy are another matter: and too often they perceive our global world of markets and consumerism as a kind of anarchy that excludes them. They yearn first of all for self-governance: the right to determine some portion of the fate they and their families and neighbors will have to endure, they may be less sanguine about their opportunities. Hence, while addressing global anarchy and moving to democratize global affairs will not end terrorism, it will make such violence far more aberrant, far less seductive to third world masses who currently count themselves as among the powerless and the marginalized.

There are two democratic deficiencies worth noting, deficiencies that make many people feel like they already live in the state of nature where there is neither safety nor liberty, neither justice nor equality to be had. The first is America's (and the West's) democratic deficit: our failure to live up to our aspirations, to encompass and include all of our citizens in the noble formula promising liberty to all. The second is the global democratic deficit: the absence of democratic regulatory and legal institutions at the global level to contain and domesticate the anarchy of international markets, an anarchy that serves terrorism all too well. Democracy within our system is one subtext and global-ization and its impact on democracy internationally is the other.

On the way to taking up these two already complex themes, I will have to simplify how I treat culture and religion. I will confound them unashamedly in this analysis, fully aware that a more careful study would have to disentangle them, distinguishing a national or ethnic culture from a religious or value culture (though the two obviously intersect). I will employ a shorthand for now, asking your indulgence for not doing all of the careful work of good social science at the same moment. When I say culture, I will mean religion and when I say reli-gion I will mean culture. And I know I will be wrong in obvious ways on both counts.

Our Democratic Deficit

If the war of the fundamentalists against modernity, of what I have called Jihad vs. McWorld, is not to be understood (as observers like Samuel Huntington and Andrew Sullivan have mistakenly under-stood it) as a rude clash among and betwen civilizations in which Islam, hijacked by its fundamentalists, is trying to push the modern world back into the Middle Ages, then it must be understood as a clash within cultures, a clash within a single modern civilization. There is a fundamentalist tendency inside of all religions: we did not have to go back to the Crusades or the Inquisition to be treated to a Christian version by American Taliban like Jerry Falwell right after September 11, attributing the attack to a wrathful God seeking ven-gence on gays, abortionists, feminists, and the American Civil Liberties Union.

This tendency is exacerbated by the aggressively secular and shamelessly materialistic tendencies of modernity's global markets and its pervasive, privatizing attachment to consumerism. When it becomes too hard to find a venue for religious devotionals and prayer in modern society's secularized venues (the multiplex, the TV room, the computer lab), some will seek instead a venue for religious martyrdom. When worship cannot be undertaken peacefully it will transform itself into a great "struggle" for purification—a "Jihad" against infidels whose infidelity is not the worship of another religion but the rejection of all religions and the crass cultivation of a secular cultural imperialism.

Fundamentalism is in fact an invention of the West, of Christianity: the Crusaders were the first great Jihadic warriors bent on punishing infidels and establishing a realm of God as defined by one of his intolerant congregations. Unsatisfied with its wars on Islam (which Christianity lost, as Islamic Jihad will surely lose its Crusade today), Christianity fell to confessional internecine bickering and, in time, fratricidal war that culminated in the Thirty Years' War, which was organized around a sectarian struggle for religious purity, and decimated the European population.

What Europe discovered (and Islam had yet fully to appreciate) is that the coexistence of religion and secular sovereignty demands a division in the human soul: a portioning out of those things that are spiritual to the Church, and those that are worldly, to the State. Pope Gelasius, still deep in the Middle Ages, posited a doctrine of the Two Swords in which religion and the state were to keep each to its own realm, segmenting the work of the body and the work of the soul. The two swords doctrine recognized implicitly that when the state encroached on the realm of the spirit there was a danger of political tyranny, what we today call political totalitarianism; and when the church encroached on the realm of the body there was the danger of theocracy, intolerance, and civil strife.

The two swords solution avoided both anarchy and tyranny, but it left the deeply religious malcontent. And as they felt their dwindling realm pinched by modernity—by secularism, privatization, and commerce—they revolted against the prudence of separation and the liberal dogmas of boundaries, which might have been a protection for a modest secularism in deeply religious times but became a treat to religion in deeply secular times. Puritans attempted a commonwealth in Massachusetts, and today their great grandchildren, who are now parents, draw their own children out of public schools, appalled by the invasive popular culture. Jewish fundamentalists rejected the state of Israel as a sacrilege against the call of the spirit, while others also in the name of fundamentalist dogmas today lay claim to lands in Palestine ("Judea and Sumaria") that were not part of the state of Israel. Recently empowered Hindi fundamentalists insist the state impose the authority of religion on wayward souls, and are a threat to religious pluralism in democratic India.

It is then hardly a surprise or a break with tradition that a handful of the children of Islam, speaking on behalf of an impoverishment and occupation they themselves do not necessarily suffer, imagine that the new global disorder spells the death of their children, their values and their religion. Those twisted by their beliefs into a war on innocence and a race to martyrdom, must be interdicted by force: but let us not imagine that this will suffice to arrest the spread of fundamentalism or to cure the world of pathological terrorism. We need to address not only poverty but the question of a venue for religious practice. In the US we have extended the reasonable argument on behalf of the separation of church and state into an unreasonable argument about the necessity of privatizing religion. Religion is by definition public in its essence: it pertains to communities and congregations, not merely individuals, and its practice entails public norms. To insulate it from the state (and the state from it) cannot be to call for its privatization. Islam in its current fundamentalist variation may seek too much public room, but Christianity and other religions have been compelled to occupy too little. And so, understandably, the deeply religious chafe at the restrictions.

If fundamentalists exist in every religion and represent a reaction to liberal boundaries too crudely enforced and separations of domain too dogmatically imposed (often without reference to consumerism's boundary-crossing ambitions), they can also be found in cultural and ethnic communities where it is appropriate to speak of cultural fundamentalism. Here too women and men who feel they are under assault make claims about the dominion of ethnicity that can appear totalizing and exclusivist. Former Yugoslavia imploded around fissures created by an intersection of religious and ethnic fundamentalisms for which genocide turned out to be the only response. Many Americans like Jeremy Rifkin embrace the term "culture," forgetting that it has often (especially in Europe) been a repository for dangerous, politically insidious, and deeply undemocratic tendencies.

There are to be sure open and tolerant cultures and communities, but there are also closed, exclusive, and intolerant communities; it is not a novel argument to suggest that the stronger a community becomes, the more coherent and integral its culture, the less tolerant and open it is likely to be. Communities rooted in common culture offer many of the features we yearn for in seeking a cultural identity: fraternity, a sense of belonging, homogeneity, common ground—such (and here is the rub) as might be afforded by the Ku Klux Klan or the

Montana Militia or by Islamic Jihad. Thick, strong communities of culture are far more rewarding than thin associational networks like the Sierra Club or the American Civil Liberties Union or Medecins sans frontieres. Paying dues to a distant association that puts into practice a few of your values cannot stir the soul the way that belonging to and acting on behalf of a band of brothers tied together by a struggle (Jihad?) for (or against) justice can.

There is a natural and unavoidable tension then between the values of cultural community and the values of an open society, between identity and democracy. Citizenship is democracy's identity, but it is less robust than say race or religion. To believe otherwise is wishful thinking. To democratize our cultural communities inevitably weakens them, though it renders them far less vulnerable to abuse and far more compatible with progressive liberal ideals. We make them thinner precisely in order to weaken their hold on imagination. A youth hiking club, let alone the Sierra Club, will not bind its members the way the Hitler Jugend did—thank goodness. Identity politics turns out not to be very good for democray, even though democracy needs secure, culturally identified members.

No American can resist the seductive civic language of Alexis de Tocqueville who captured the local vitality of democracy in America in its infant form: strong local communities constituted by engaged citizens. Engaged male citizens. Engaged male, white, Protestant, property-owning citizens. Ask any woman, any African-American, about the vitality of American democracy in the 1830's when Tocqueville made his deftly chronicled journey. "Democracy for whom?" they will ask. "Not for us." The robustness of the municipality celebrated by Tocqueville was in fact purchased by exclusion and homogeneity. By slavery and the disenfranchisement of women. Our citizen body today is far more inclusive, far more encompassing, far more diverse. But less engaged, less possessed of common values, less able to identify as a singular community. The bargain we made in America was to surrender a robust but narrowly based and exclusionary civic engagement and municipal liberty on behalf of an inclusive multicultural society as civically wan as it was civically free— emancipated from slavery but distanced also from common ground. The American Southland before the Civil War was in fact, as any reader of that great American pop classic "Gone with the Wind" knows, home to an aristocratic and deeply American culture in which family, church, and community were perhaps more firmly entrenched than anywhere else in America. At the price of slavery and the subjugation of women to proud manners. As a community, the South was far superior to the new industrial cities of the North, where proletarians were economically worse off than some house slaves.

In short, as we take on the Taliban in Afghanistan and terrorists in Iraq, we need to examine our own civic souls. Before we dismiss their cries of "hypocrisy" when we boast of our liberties, we need to examine our history and our civic institutions. We are not wrong in our pride of democracy, and they are not right in their narrow-minded intolerance of pluralism and freedom. But we need to get our democratic practices right and real in order to effectively challenge their antidemocratic rhetoric. We need not embrace Huntington's notion of a clash of civilizations: our own contains all the tensions and contradictions he attributes to the "other." We have our own demons sitting on our left shoulder, arguing with the better angels perched on the right. Lincoln knew we did not have to look in foreign lands and distant cultures for the roots of our problems in our own great civil war. He knew we would pay in blood for the injustices committed in the name of our liberties.

American Exceptionalism and the End
of American Innocence

To capture our own democratic deficit we need only problematize our own claims to democracy. This is not to surrender our ideals but to reenforce them by being frank about the challenges they faced and face in light of our own history. The global democratic deficit is not a matter of aspirations incompletely realized, however, but about a project wholly unbegun. In America we have used a myth of American exceptionalism to insulate ourselves from our responsibilities to and in the world. As the Swiss label themselves "Sonderfall Schweiz" we insist we are "Sonderfall America"—a mythic land of new beginnings where it is impossible to retrieve the innocence of Eden, a "City on the Hill" where as Tom Paine insisted, we could go back to the beginning of time and start the world over again. The history of violence, mischief, and malevolence, the contradictions, errors, and prejudices of Europe that Voltaire and the Enlightenment philosophs had already identified as synonymous with European history could be eluded, evaded, pushed aside. Protected by two great oceans and our own "pure" origins, this would be the land of "new men," a land of innocence and renewal, a literal "tabula rasa" on which a new history could be inscribed. (In reality of course America already had a native population that would in time be removed from the land, and its proud new constitution acknowledged and perpetuated slavery, but these were small things in the face of so large a myth.)

The myth of innocence depended of course on the myth of independence—of autonomy, separation, and absolute national sovereignty. Geography and history (or its absence) were the guarantors of the new isolation of America from the world. Well into the twentieth century, American foreign policy was organized around the attempt to insulate and protect America from the world. And when in the twentieth century we finally had to go to foreign soil to wage foreign wars, we understood ourselves as intervening good-naturedly in other people's conflagrations. Star Wars (the missile shield in its latest variation) is only the last effort in the attempt to construct a virtual ocean through technology that will keep us from our foreign enemies.

September 11 spelled the end of the twin myths of American innocence and American independence. The terrorists made a mockery of sovereignty. Theirs was a lesson in malevolent interdependence enforced by terror and underscored by fear. With the falling towers fell also the conceit that it is possible for any nation to go it alone in the new world of anarchic interdependence. America can try to stay out of the world, but the world will not stay out of America. There are no oceans wide enough, no shields strong enough, no walls high enough to protect it from the repercussions of global anarchy. The world came to America in the incarnation that had always occupied our nightmares—as men of evil risen up from amongst us to strike us down. The "evil ones" may have once been trained in Eygpt or Sudan or Afghanistan, but they were living not in Cairo or Hamburg or Kabul but in Florida and New Jersey, and training in American schools, learning American skills, embracing American technologies, and hiding behind American habits of tolerance, pluralism, and privacy they intended by their deeds to assault and destroy.

This should not have come as such a shock. America is a remarkably multicultural country, as "global" a society as exists within any single nation on earth. The world as defined by its many peoples had already come to America long before September 11, and those peoples brought with them their many distinctive virtues and vices, their pleasures and resentments, their yearnings for opportunity and their yearnings for annihilation. Interdependence was the American reality long before the World Trade Center attack brought the reality home to the great American majority. But the reality had been defied by a hubristically unilateralist foreign policy that conspired through neglect and isolation in a global anarchy that fostered free markets and rampant terrorism alike. The refusal to pay UN dues, the walk out from UNESCO (the UN's educational, scientific, and cultural organization), the rejection of the Land Mines Ban Treaty and the Kyoto Protocol on Global Warming, the disdain for the terrror negotiations and refusal to participate in the Durban Conference on racism (misguided and biased as it might have been) were all manfestations of what even to America's friends seemed an American arrogance that was as foolish as it was counterproductive.

But September 11, a day of terror, reminded the American nation that an anarchic world could push America itself back into a state of nature where insecurity was ubiquitous and fear the only engine of social relations. As once the state of nature (as a metaphor for the chaos of the religious wars and the anarchy of nation-building in France and England) had been the philosophical context for the legitimation of powerful new democratic forms of sovereignty (all political authority is rooted in the consent of the governed, which is given to the state in return for a guarantee of liberty and order), so again today global anarchy beckons new forms of global sovereignty capable of securing tranquility in the face of terror.

The question is, in response to the now acknowledged global anarchy, will the US attempt to distinguish between the anarchy that drives global markets and the anarchy that drives terrorists, and deal only with the latter through military and intelligence means, imposing a Pax America on the world that is merely an attempt to extend American sovereignty rather than recognize its limits? Or will it grasp that interdependence means the anarchy of global markets and the anarchy of terrorism are linked, and that an appropriate response to them must be to find ways to globalize sovereignty and its defining democratic institutions? The choice is clear, the American preference is not. Both positions are represented within the Bush administration and within the American people. Those who insist, in the President's rhetoric, that the world choose sides—that it join the US or be numbered among the supporters of terrorism—are traditionalists clinging to the hope that America can still make it alone, as long as others follow in its path. The alternative is for America to join the world, to become a leading partner in multilateral negotiations acknowledging differences and the vital interests of other nations, which may not coincide exactly with our own. US Secretary of State Colin Powell's prudent coalition-building approach has pursued this model. President Bush himself has courted both camps, though in the long term the two are not coherent or compatible.

The War of All against All and the International Disorder

Either way, the war of all against all will have to be confronted in the global setting. And that means the democratization of globalization: the introduction of some form of popular sovereignty and civic participation in the anarchic international domain. The alternative is Hobbes's war of all against all, in which force and fraud are the cardinal virtues (something al Qaeda seems to understand all too well). After all, Hobbes' first law of nature is to do all that is necessary to survive, and that includes the "right" to kill others.

The contradiction faced by the US is then that it has itself quite consciously conspired in the creation of an international "order" that is actually an international disorder—a contrived war of all against all posturing as a free market but establishing conditions as favorable to the globalization of crime, weapons, prostitution, drugs, and terror as to the the spread of unregulated markets. An invisible trade-off has been made that secures highly profitable free markets—an unregulated and opaque interdependence, dominated by wholly unregulated transnational financial and corporate interests—at the price of a global environment conducive to a far more malevolent interdependence dominated by criminals and terrorists. In what amounts to a radically asymmetrical form of internationalism, Americans and their allies have globalized the economy, globalized trade, globalized the free movement of human and natural resources, and globalized the many vices associated with free markets as well. But they have not globalized the democratic, legal, and civic institutions that within nation-states contain and regulate capitalism and its free market institutions and prevent anarchy from prevailing.

Capitalism is a tiger, full of vitality and strength that can be tapped to energize an economy—if the tiger is caged and its energies domesticated by civic and political institutions. Globalization has let the tiger out of the cage, however, setting free a "wild" capitalism, which, like a tiger set free, has resumed its predatory and all-consuming habits.

Wild power can only be tamed by a social contract and the imposition of popular sovereignty. The question is whether this is possible at the global level; and whether the US will now join efforts to make it possible. As this once meant that individuals had to yield their unbounded liberty to act as they pleased in return for a gurantee of their actual safety and a now somewhat more limited but secure liberty, states too will have to make this bargain, allowing their sovereignty to be encroached upon in the name of a new global security. We can no longer pick and choose between anarchies, content to embrace the economic anarchy of unregulated markets, but appalled by the political anarchy bred by global terrorism. International disorder serves one and all alike. It affords freedom to corporations to dominate the economic sector without fear of regulation or containment; and it affords freedom to terrorists to work the interstices of the anarchic interdependence that is the global disorder. Indeed, terror is the pathological expression of a resentment and despair far more widely felt by those abused and marginalized by the anarchy of global market relations. Americans ask "Why do they hate us?" The victims of the global economic disorder do not hate America, but they want their pain and suffering to count as much as the pain and suffering of those who were slaughtered on September 11. Their goal is not to trivialize or deprecate America's suffering but to dramatize their own, though theirs is less "newsworthy" and dramatic, being spread over months or years, with casualties expiring slowly of disease, starvation, and penury.

The social contracts of earlier ages often involved a declaration of independence in which a people announced their autonomy and sovereignty from domestic tyrants or foreign overlords. They belonged to an era of nation building in which the establishing and defense of borders was crucial. Ours is a new age in which borders have grown porous and the global social contract calls for a novel and unprecedented Declaration of Interdependence. Nation by nation, democracy can no longer survive. Because capitalism was a global system, Trotsky grasped long ago that "socialism in one country" was not possible. Because economics and ecology and technology and culture, no less than crime and disease and revolution and terrorism, compel a new global system, we must understand that "democracy in one country" is no longer possible either. Hobbes' contradiction, that to overcome anarchy within nations, one had to create a sovereign nation-state system in which there would be anarchy among nations, can no longer stand. The costs have become too high, leaving the predators of international anarchy to feed not just on individual states but the nation-state system itself. The call today for the globalization of democracy, the globalization of law, the construction of strong international institutions that allow genuine participation, is no longer simply a romantic call of irrelevant world federalists for an impossible utopia. It has become an issue of national security, an imperative of a new realism. Here we come full circle to the argument I started with—Why are people throwing bombs inside a democracy (even if they are outside the democracy)?

The answer would seem to be that for those who support resistance and acquiesce to terrorism there is no democracy. A social contract that does not include every people and every nation cannot work. To tame terrorism means to tame the anarchism within which corporations and global financial capital have found it comfortable to operate. Yet not only has the West failed to create a global order that contains financial anarchism, it has nurtured an ideology—some would say a theology—of privatization that has actually advocated less public accountability, less transparency and less democracy within nations. The neoliberal paradigm advocated by Reagan and Thatcher and embraced now even by parties of the "left" began by making war on "big government" and its bureaucratic unresponsiveness, but it has today become less an assault on government than an attack on the *res publica*, the public things and goods that define democracy. To privatize has come to mean, quite literally, to publicize goods, taking them out of the public domain and leaving the civic community without a foundation. With a sense of our publicness, we lose any possibility of common ground.

Only after September 11 did the Western public rather abruptly recomprehend the meaning of public goods. Many people who had not thought about the *res publica* for a long time noticed that public safety and national security were goods that could and should not be privatized. No one called Bill Gates of Microsoft or Michael Eisner of Disney on September 12 asking for a strategy to respond to terrorism. On the contrary, politicians who long advocated dismantling government pushed hard to "federalize" American airport security workers who were privately owned, badly paid, undertrained, and as a consequence, through no fault of their own, utterly incompetent. Public workers—policemen, firemen, and security officials, suddenly became heroes, displacing stockbrokers, lawyers, and bankers as the indispensable men and women of a society under siege. Consumers no longer dominated our world: citizenship regained its power to kindle hope and inspiration: the citizen-cop, the citizen-soldier, the citizen-President embodying the spirit of a people who abruptly recognized the meaning of their commonality.

More than anything else, the aftermath of September 11 has renewed the need for and importance of civic faith, that *"Verfassungspatriotismus"* as Habermas has dubbed it, that secular ideology of high ideals that holds otherwise disparate elements of a multicultural nation together. America's civil religion has been its greatest civic asset over its two hundred year history. The ubiquitous American flag may seem to observers outside the US to be but a sentimental and even dangerous token of national jingoism, but to many Americans it is an emblem of national unity and a reminder of what binds Americans together as a democratic people. It imparts to the thin identity of citizenship a much thicker identity of civic membership in what the pragmatist philosopher John Dewey called "the great community." It represents allegiance to a social contract founded on popular sovereignty, recalling Americans to the need for democracy in security both liberty and safety.

If we are to construct a global order that is as just as it is productive, as immune to economic exploitation as to terrorist nihilism, as protective of women and children as it is of property, then what will be required are not only new democratic and civic institutions, but some form of a global civic faith around which transnational citizenship can be established.

At its inception, Europe was not a prospective economic union or tariff zone, it was an idea that men like Jean Monnet dreamed from the ashes of too many wars. It was the idea of the European—which sadly today has been diminished to the idea of the Euro. Yet there is today an emerging European civil religion, a European point of view, a sense of European identity for which a currency union is only a weak symbol.

Global Civil Society and a Place for Religion

To create a just and inclusive world in which all citizens are stakeholders is the first objective of a rational strategy against terrorism, but a civil religion that imposes secularism or appears hostile to religion will not be adequate to the crisis of fundamentalism. For adversaries of the West are not only seeking to share in the bounty of capitalism but to attenuate its secularist force and its totalizing materialism. They worry that global capitalism will prosper without them or at their expense, but they also worry that it will manage to include them and thereby undermine their values and corrupt their children. "McWorld" brings a world of ambivalence with it, and its potential success in including them is as worrisome as its actual failure to do so.

The neoliberal myth of omnipotent markets has created a novel bottom-up form of totalizing homogeneity that is deeply threatening to religious diversity and the pursuit of nonmaterial goods, whether cultural, educational, or religious. Christian fundamentalists have been as outspoken in their fear of pop cultural materialism and its attachment to titillating material overload and violence as Muslim and Jewish fundamentalists. Millions of American Christians home-school their children to keep them from the pop culture that pervades public education. Muslim parents who are peaceful and hardworking can nonetheless see in the totalizing onslaught of material con-sumerism a threat to their most cherished values.

It is one of the conundrums of our day that when religion is per-mitted to dominate every sector of life, we call it theocracy and com-plain about tyranny; and when a one-party state dominates every sector of life, we call it totalitarianism, and complain about the destruction of liberty; but when economics and the private material sector dominates every sector of life, we call it freedom and celebrate the triumph of the one-dimensional market society. A global civic faith will have to make room for matters of the spirit as well as the needs of the body. It will have to assure pluralism as well as privacy and guarantee that "free" markets do not undermine the conditions of real freedom. These are tasks that go beyond the building of global institutions of economic oversight and the regulation of social justice. But they are as important to the defeat of terrorism as the economic and political agenda.

A proper place for religion in a new and just global order will require that we revisit the compromises of the earlier social contract tra-dition. When religion was allowed to dominate politics as it did in the centuries prior to the rise of democracy, there were endless civil wars rooted in pervasive intolerance and religious absolutism. Regimes of tolerance requires the separation of religion from governance, and the social compacts of the sixteenth and seventeenth centuries pushed reli-gion away from the state, most notably in the legal separation of the two domains in America's founding constitutional document. The compact called for a priority of identities in which people would agree to be citizens first and believers only afterwards; in return, citizens would assure both the noninterference of the state in the choice of religions and the free practice of every religious faith.

The compromise worked well as long as societies were fairly religious and the state was the securer of free religious practice rather than its enemies. But in the era of McWorld, which is a secular theology in its own right with an aggressive secular faith in material production and consumption as the key to the good life, believers and worshipers have felt pushed aside, even in America, and certainly in the rest of the world. In recent years, the courts in the US have treated the separation of church and state as an argument for the wholesale privatization of religion—turning it from a public but nonstate affair of the community into a private matter of personal preference for the home. But religion isn't a private preference like television viewing choices. Nobody can practice religion in the privacy of the home. A church is a community of worshipers and participates in public practices that depend on public venues.

Out of respect for religious differences, Americans have banned religious symbols from public places. This robs religion of its venue; it protects the minority but removes from the majority its capacity to celebrate its community beliefs as a community. At the global level, a way needs to be found to prevent an official religion without privatizing religious communities. We cannot secure the liberty of the public square by driving the faithful of every religion from it. Civil society at its best is that nonstate public realm where through free association we create the voluntary communities of education, culture, and faith that define our plural human character. Civil society is not coercive but it is public; it is free, but it is not private. It demands adequate space for all those activities that give meaning and dignity to life.

To respond adequately to those left out of the global disorder by its anarchy and its vulnerability to the powerful, the rich and the violent, it must then first of all be a civic space. That means neither government nor markets can alone be its creators. It means that the new global social contract, rooted in a new declaration of interdependence, will have as much room for religion as for markets, and a civic space as robust and free as its democratic government. That is a tall order of course. But it is by far the best way to offer a future to those who live today without hope for justice or for the survival of their most deeply held religious values. By bringing all humankind within the sphere of democracy, and constructing a compact that overcomes the anarchy of global relations, we make a world in which both liberty and faith are secured, and in which, as a consequence, terrorism becomes irrelevant. For in a living public square with polling booth and parliaments and free media on one side and places of worship and schools and civil associations on the other, with factories and shops open to all in the middle, there will be no need for anyone to throw bombs. Life under these conditions will be too good to allow even zealots to fall in love with death.

Index

About the Editor and Contributors

Benjamin R. Barber is the Gershon and Carol Kekst Professor of Civil Society at the University of Maryland and a principal of the Democracy Collaborative. He brings an abiding concern for democracy and citizenship to issues of politics, culture, and education in America and abroad. Barber consults regularly with political and civic leaders in the United States and Europe. His honors include Guggenheim, Fulbright, and Social Science Research Fellowships, the Palmes Academiques (Chevalier) of the French Government, and the Berlin Prize of the American Academy of Berlin. He was founding editor, and for ten years editor, of *Political Theory*. Barber's fifteen books include the classic, *Strong Democracy* (1984), *Jihad vs. McWorld* (1995), and *The Truth of Power: Intellectual Affairs in the Clinton White House* (2002).

Lloyd J. Dumas is Professor of Economics and Political Economy at the School of Social Sciences, University of Texas (Dallas). He has published over one hundred works in eleven languages in books and journals of economics, engineering, sociology, history, public policy, military studies, and peace science, as well as in newspapers and magazines. He has participated in numerous conferences and special lectures since 1980, including serving as co-organizer (with Ali Mazrui) of an International Conference on Peacekeeping, Development, and

Demilitarization in Africa, sponsored by the Rockefeller Foundation and the U.S. Institute of Peace. In addition, Dumas has addressed the United Nations, and served as Vice Chair of the Texas Governor's Task Force on Economic Transition, and as a consultant to the Los Alamos National Laboratories. He is the author of six books, including *Lethal Arrogance: Human Fallibility and Dangerous Technologies* (St. Martin's Press, 1999).

Robert K. Fullinwider is research scholar at the Institute for Philosophy and Public Policy at the School of Public Affairs, University of Maryland. Among other topics, he has written on military conscription, affirmative action, war, multicultural education, professional ethics, and moral learning. He is editor of *Public Education in a Multicultural Society* (1996), and *Civil Society, Democracy and Civic Renewal* (1999). His book *The Reverse Discrimination Controversy* (1980) was a selection of the Lawyer's Literary Guild. Fullinwider is now co-authoring a book on college admissions. During 1996–1998, he was research director for the National Commission on Civic Renewal, a joint project of the Institute for Philosophy and Public Policy and the Pew Charitable Trusts.

William A. Galston is director of the Institute for Philosophy and Public Policy and professor at the School of Public Affairs, University of Maryland. Galston also serves as director of the Center for Information and Research on Civic Learning and Engagement (CIRCLE). He is a political theorist who both studies and participates in American politics and domestic policy. He was deputy assistant to the president for Domestic Policy, 1993–1995, and executive director of the National Commission on Civic Renewal, 1996–1999. Galston served as a founding member of the Board of the National Campaign to Prevent Teen Pregnancy and as chair of the campaign's task force on religion and public values. He is the author of five books and nearly one hundred articles in moral and political theory, American politics, and public policy. His publications include *Liberal Purposes* (Cambridge, 1991) and *Liberal Pluralism* (Cambridge, 2002).

Verna V. Gehring is editor at the Institute for Philosophy and Public Policy at the School of Public Affairs, University of Maryland. She is a philosopher broadly interested in the obligations of state and citizen, and the various accounts of civil society. In addition to her work on the seventeenth-century political philosopher Thomas Hobbes and his enduring influence, Gehring's interest is applied to such contemporary matters as the state lottery, nuclear proliferation, and computer hackers. She serves as editor of *Philosophy & Public Policy Quarterly*, reviewer of ethics manuscripts for Oxford University Press, and moderator for the Aspen Institute. She is coeditor, with William A. Galston, of *Philosophical Dimensions of Public Policy* (2002).

Paul W. Kahn is Robert W. Winner Professor of Law and the Humanities, and director of the Orville H. Schell Jr. Center for Human Rights at Yale Law School. He served as a law clerk to Justice White in the United States Supreme Court from 1980 to 1982. Before coming to Yale Law School in 1985 he practiced law in Washington, D.C. He teaches in the areas of constitutional law and theory, international law, and philosophy. He is author of *Legitimacy and History: Self-Government in American Constitutional Theory* (1992), *The Reign of Law: Marbury v. Madison and the Construction of America* (1997), *The Cultural Study of Law: Reconstructing Legal Scholarship* (1999), *Law and Love: The Trials of King Lear* (2000), and many articles.

Judith Lichtenberg is associate professor in the Department of Philosophy, and research scholar at the Institute for Philosophy and Public Policy, University of Maryland. Since 1998 she has served as director of the Committee on Politics, Philosophy, and Public Policy, an interdisciplinary graduate program. Her research interests within ethics and political philosophy include higher education, race and ethnicity, international ethics, and media ethics. She is editor of *Democracy and the Mass Media* (1990), and the author of many articles.

David Luban is Frederick Haas Professor of Law and Philosophy at Georgetown University Law Center. He has written or edited five books, including *Legal Modernism* (1994) and *Lawyers and Justice: An Ethical Study* (1998), and has published many articles on legal and philosophical topics. Before coming to Georgetown, Professor Luban taught for seventeen years at the University of Maryland School of Law, where he was also a member of the Institute for Philosophy and Public Policy. He has taught at the Harvard and Yale Law Schools, and the philosophy departments of Dartmouth College, Kent State University, and the University of Melbourne, and Yale.